First Rate Living

In God's Company

First Rate Living

In God's Company

David A. Stone

ISBN 978-1-105-13754-9

To my mother, Nella K. Stone (January 1, 1924–December 21, 2009). Follower of Christ, devoted wife to Frederic A. Stone, loving mother of five sons, open with her opinions, and always in charge.

Acknowledgments

Trina: my life partner, co-founder of First Rate, Inc., and my best friend! Allan, Preston & Kathryn: my three kids and my best mirrors of God's grace and mercy. Dr. Frederic A. Stone, Col. (Ret. USAF): my dad and best man. Allen, Brian, Judson, and Stephen: my birth brothers and best "quit crying, you baby" encouragers. Honey and Doc Bruner: Trina's parents and my best supporters. Stephen Bruner: my brother-in-law and best summertime co-worker on the farm. Curtiss Rooks, Dave Brown, and Andy Kline: my college roommates, teammates, and best lifelong friends. Jim Earl Swilley: first personal pastor and my best Bible teacher. Jimmy Weatherford: my "man friend" married to Trina's "woman friend," Marcy, and my best friend. (I miss you!) Brian Thompson, Jeanne Benson, Deb Repak, Kate Baird, and Craig Wietz: "God family in performance" and my best lifelong co-workers. Lonnie Hayter: life pastor and my best "life's a messy business" brother in Christ. Tim and Lydia McKibben: marriage, business, and spiritual mentors and my best givers. John Watkins: first hire at First Rate, Inc. and my best application programmer. Darryl Gabehart, L. J. Adams, and Craig Porter: co-owned a boat with us and my best family life buddies. Sean Lambert: first mission mentor and my best apostolic pioneer leader. Muhammed Fahim: first Afghan co-worker and my best Afghan brother. Steve James, Eric Affeldt, Howard Getson, and Jamie Waller: my First Rate board of advisors and my best coaches. Bill Butterworth: speaker, writer, and my best book buddy. First Rate, Inc. employees: creating a God-centered business legacy and my best co-workers in the world! It's all about relationships for me. God moves in relationship. I am sorry I cannot name everyone that God has moved through in my life. Thank you for loving, giving, serving, and enjoying life with me! That's First Rate Living!

Contents

John Wayne or Mr. Rogers

"I don't know what you think you're saying to me, Dad," Al explained, "but I'll tell you what I am hearing."

"What is it?" I replied. I was angry with my son, but tried my best to hold it in and listen to his reasoning.

"Two things. The first one is that you think I'm a loser and that I will never amount to anything."

I was stunned. Never ever had I meant to communicate that sort of message to my son. He meant everything to me.

"There's another message I'm getting from you, too," Al added. "You take pride in the fact that you have a company you're running that is all about love and family," he paused, "but, Dad, you have a real family that sucks."

His words stung. Why had he picked up on messages that I never intended to give? Something was wrong and I had to do some correcting.

Al was in the seventh grade when this encounter occurred. He was a gifted athlete. He loved football and excelled at it, but his junior high school had a policy that stated if you failed just one class you would be declared ineligible to participate in sports. In a move I could not understand, Al had managed to fail a class, thus setting up this conversation. The teachers at his school had a general idea of what was going on. They had seen these symptoms before.

"Your son isn't doing well in my class," the teacher explained. "And without saying it in so many words, he is blaming you," he continued as he pointed his finger directly at me. I could almost feel it push into me.

"Me? He's blaming me?"

"Yes, Mr. Stone, that's the way I interpret it."

It was that conversation that led us to seek out the school counselor. After a couple visits, she gave me some homework. "There is a book I recommend to parents who are in situations like the one you're in," she told me. "It's called *Bright Minds, Poor*

Grades, and the author is Michael Whitley. I think you ought to get yourself a copy and read it very carefully."

In no time I had the book in my possession. This entire issue was not only devastating to Al—it was devastating to me. As I read Whitley's book, I began to see myself in his descriptions of certain kinds of parents. He distinguishes between two types of parenting styles. The first is strong, almost military-like, which Dr. Whitley refers to as the John Wayne approach to parenting. I had never really thought of myself in those terms, but the more I read his description, the more I had to admit, that was my style.

The opposite approach was that of a kind, loving, more approachable type of parent. Whitley chooses to call this style the Mr. Rogers type of parenting. Lots of folks have made fun of Fred Rogers over the years, but I knew that down deep we all realized this kind, gentle man had a natural way of letting children know how much they were truly loved, valued, and affirmed.

As I read the book, the underlying message hit me over the head like a two-by-four. I needed to make the necessary changes to be less like John Wayne and more like Mr. Rogers. It was a much needed wake-up call and thank God it came while I still had some time with my precious son.

In a subsequent conversation with a close friend, I remember admitting to the many mistakes I had made as a parent and reassuring him that I was trying to make the proper corrections in order to be a better parent.

"Dave, I have a question to ask you," he said. "If something horrible happened to you and your wife, so that Al would end up on the street as a twelve-year-old, do you think he would make it?"

I thought for only a moment and replied, "Yes, I know he would make it."

"Well, then parent that way. Parent him like he's going to make it."

He let the gravity of those words sink in for a minute before he began again. "You know, Dave, Al has the desire to be just like you. That is his greatest wish."

"No, no," I protested. "All he talks about around the house is Dennis Rodman." Back in those days, Rodman was the Bad Boy of the Chicago Bulls, playing alongside Scotty Pippen and the great Michael Jordan. For some unexplained reason, Al was fascinated with his style and manner of play.

"Dennis Rodman may be who he is talking about," my friend explained, "but the role model on his mind is you."

This is how I began my journey to be a good father as well as a successful businessman. It wasn't enough to be wonderful on stage. I wanted success backstage with those who knew me the best. I learned how to move from control to influence. I took a familiar quotation from the Lord Jesus and rewrote it to clarify my goal:

What does it profit a man if he gains a successful business, but loses his own family?

Over the subsequent years, I have worked hard at putting both portions of my life together in a package that I have come to call First Rate Living. That's what this book is all about—what it looks like and how I got there. It's a story of faith in the workplace, but it goes much deeper. It's about every aspect of life. This book is for people trying to grow their influence, not their control. I have a fun side and I have a serious side, but all in all, I'm just a plain old guy.

Later that year, I took Al shopping for basketball shoes. He needed some new ones. I was accompanying him to hang out and, of course, to pay. When we arrived at the store, we were overwhelmed with dozens of possibilities. The most popular basketball shoes were named after NBA stars, and I couldn't help but notice there was a pair named for the Bad Boy himself, Dennis Rodman.

I moved in that direction, thinking Al would be right behind me. Surely he had seen the signs showing us the way to the high-priced shoes, but to my surprise, Al left my side and gravitated to a different part of the store. I decided to not say anything in order to watch the scene play out. After careful scrutiny, Al brought over his choice. I was dumbfounded by his decision. They were not Rodman's—that was unmistakable. They were just the opposite. Al held a pair of plain, white Nike basketball shoes. That's right, plain white. No stripes, no color, no tie-in to an NBA legend.

I guess an ordinary pair of shoes better symbolized Al's role model. Maybe a little bit more like Mr. Rogers would wear.

It certainly caused me to take a look at where this John Wayne-turned-Mr. Rogers guy had come from. So let's step back a bit and see how this story all started.

Band of Brothers and Military Moves

I am the youngest of five boys. My four older brothers are approximately one year apart from each other. Then there was a four-year gap. Then me.

My most vivid, recurring childhood memory played out when I was around nine years old. My parents went out on Friday nights for a dinner date. With so many older brothers, they never considered hiring a babysitter, so I was left home in the care of my brothers. Every time they left, I would stand at the front door, crying, pleading with my mom and dad, "Please don't leave me here. I'm gonna die! They'll kill me!"

And they would chuckle, pat me on the head, and leave. For the next two or three hours, the five of us would fight like there was no tomorrow. Since I was the youngest, I always seemed to get the worst of it.

Being four years younger than the next youngest brother was quite an adventure. When I say they were always beating me up, I am, of course, over-generalizing. But it seemed like if they weren't beating me up, then they were trying their best to leave me behind. They left me at as many places as they could dream up. When I thought it couldn't get any worse, Mom and Dad left me at church one Sunday. I was in the second grade.

"Where's Dave?" someone finally asked that late Sunday afternoon in Fairfield, California.

"I don't know—did you bring him home with you, dear?" my perplexed Mom asked my confused Dad.

"No, I thought he came home with you," Dad replied. Eventually they found me. I was sitting outside the church, waiting for my ride.

There were times when my older brothers couldn't get rid of me, so they tried an alternate method: if you hang around with us, we will make your life so miserable that next time you'll do anything to avoid being near us. One time my brother Allen was driving with a car full of his buddies—and me. They decided I was enjoying myself too much, so they grabbed me by the ankles and hung me out of the window of the backseat of the car. As an eight-year-old, I recall getting their point—I was terrified! And I learned the lesson: from that point on, I did everything in my power to never ride in the car with that crew again.

Don't misunderstand; we loved each other. We were just typical boys who would beat the tar out of each other at every available opportunity. As brothers, we'd defend each other against any outside adversary. But when it was just us, fighting among ourselves was the order of the day.

In watching my older brothers grow up, I observed four men take four very different paths in life. This felt freeing to me, for I believed I had a wider path down which I could wander. Watching my brothers was helpful. To this day I am still a keen observer of older men. I take in as much as I can from my elders. My two closest friends in Dallas/Fort Worth are both ten years older than me. Older men had, and continue to have, a large impact on my life.

My father was a career Air Force man. He was a flight surgeon, meaning he was both a doctor and a pilot. Because we were a military family, we moved around constantly. I lived in seven locations before I graduated from high school.

I was born in Long Beach, California, where my dad completed his medical residency. It was 1956. We stayed there until I was three years old, then we moved to Shaw Air Force Base in Sumter, South Carolina. We lived there for three years, until we moved to Travis Air Force Base in Fairfield, California, just outside of Sacramento. However, we only stayed for a year and a half. At seven and a half years old, my parents told me that we were moving to Gwinn, Michigan, in the Upper Peninsula, because Dad had been reassigned to K. I. Sawyer Air Force Base. We lived there until I was in the fifth grade when in the middle of the school year we relocated to Nellis Air Force Base in Las Vegas, Nevada. I completed the rest of fifth and sixth grades there. Seventh grade was back at K. I. Sawyer in Gwinn, and then I spent eighth grade in Ishpeming, Michigan, where my dad retired and went into private practice. (Ishpeming is the twin city of Neguane. They are both Indian names: one means heaven and the other means hell, and the two towns constantly argue over which means which.) Mom and Dad moved us back to Sumter, South

Carolina, after one year in Ishpeming, and I started and finished high school at Sumter High School. It was an amazing feeling beyond description to graduate from the same school I had begun four years earlier!

My parents, Fred and Nella Stone, trace their ancestry back to Boston, Massachusetts. Dad's family sailed over from England in 1635 on a ship named *The Increase*. My mother's side of the family was named Kilbourn. Her family traces its roots back to 1635 as well. Her family came from England too on a ship named *The Increase*—the same vessel as my Dad's family! It really is a small world!

When I think of my childhood, the spiritual aspect of our lives was significant. We attended church every Sunday at the base chapel. There was a Protestant service and a Catholic service. We chose the Protestant one; however, the chapel offered a variety of Protestant expressions. On some of the bases, a Lutheran chaplain led the flock. On others a Presbyterian or Episcopal or Baptist chaplain stood in the pulpit. Air Force chaplains came from all denominations, so we were exposed to many faith expressions.

But no matter what the expression or the style, every Sunday schedule included Sunday school meetings followed by the morning church service. We could count on it. We could also count on a huge Sunday dinner after church. Besides Dad and the five boys, Mom always set an extra place for an unmarried airman who would join us. I wonder what it must have felt like to be the only woman at a table of seven men who wolfed down every crumb of food set before them.

Dad was a pretty typical father of his day. He was the breadwinner, so he was gone a great deal of the time. Later in his Air Force career, he served as part of the Launch Site Rescue Team for the Apollo astronauts. He would be airborne in a helicopter, ready if needed, hovering over Cape Kennedy, Florida. When the launch was considered successful, the helicopter would land, and Dad would hop into a plane and fly back home to his usual duties on the base. He even did a ten-month tour of duty in Vietnam.

Dad was a good military man, rising to the rank of colonel. He was also a good doctor, intelligent and professional, and he had an incredible bedside manner. At home he was supportive, but in a quiet, cerebral way. There were occasions when he seemed more engaged in his work than he did at home, a manner I inherited from him until that fateful day my son Al confronted me with my hypocrisy.

Spiritually speaking, Dad accepted the Lord Jesus as his Savior in 1940 as a new recruit in the Air Force. Both he and Mom became active in an up-and-coming ministry called The Navigators. They both took their faith seriously; no doubt it was their moral compass for the decisions of their lives.

My parents loved to have fun, and in my early childhood years it seemed like most of the chaplains we encountered were Presbyterians. So I guess that made my parents fun-loving Presbyterians. (Can you say oxymoron?)

Even though I went to church every Sunday, I didn't have a personal relationship with God in my early years; instead, I went through the motions in order to keep everyone happy. But I do remember in the seventh grade that I went to and completed a catechism class taught by the Lutheran chaplain on the Sawyer Air Force Base in Gwinn, Michigan.

I remember shortly after class, my brother Jud came into my room one night and shared a pamphlet called "The Four Spiritual Laws," which had everything I needed to know about how to begin a personal relationship with the Lord Jesus. Jud did a good job of presenting the material to me. He was zealous about those issues, and he urged me to make a commitment to Christ.

"I'm not ready to do that yet, Jud," I answered honestly, to my brother's dismay.

That was a strange answer from a kid who had been brought up in church. But the next year, in eighth grade, we were assigned to write a paper on the three vocations that interested us the most. I chose a doctor, an athlete, and a pastor!

I was one of those kids who knew all the right answers to all the right questions, but I just didn't have a personal relationship with the Lord. I was good guy; I knew all the Bible stories, but I just didn't want to turn my life over to Him.

Things changed dramatically in ninth grade. We had moved to Sumter, South Carolina, from Michigan, and I immediately encountered an unfamiliar environment. In Michigan we attended an all-white school, whereas more than half of the students at Sumter High School were African-American. That fact didn't bother me in the least. Actually I made friends with my black schoolmates more easily than with my white peers. And that created a problem.

I didn't understand that at the time blacks and whites in Sumter still lived in a segregated community. The more black friends I made, the more my white friends avoided me. Consequently, when the black kids returned to their neighborhoods, I was left alone because I had fewer and fewer white friends—I felt like I had nowhere to go.

It started a period in my life where I was lonely. I felt separate from everything around me. I was looking for a friend.

Later that year the big church in town, First Baptist of Sumter, hosted a revival meeting. Bobby Richardson, the former New York Yankee great, was a member of that church and he had coaxed Billy Zeoli, president of Gospel Films, and Pat Boone to come to town for the extended meetings. After Pat sang, Billy gave a message. I don't remember everything he said, but I particularly remember him declaring, "Friendship with God is through Jesus Christ." That statement hit me right where I lived. I was lonely and I wanted a friend. Jesus was ready, willing, and able to be my friend forever, and it was an offer I could not refuse.

So when the invitation was extended, I walked down the aisle and asked Jesus to be my Savior. It was the best decision I ever made. Among the many others who walked the aisle that evening was a beautiful young lady named Trina Bruner. She too changed my life.

My commitment to Christ was the real deal. I immediately purchased a Bible. I chose The Living Bible, which in those days was wrapped in its ubiquitous lime green cover. I read it daily, got involved in the youth group at the Methodist church, and began attending a midweek Bible study.

The racial tension was still thick in 1971. For example, my dad's medical practice was one of the first in town where black and white patients all entered through the front door, instead of white people through the front door and black people through the back.

I continued to develop friendships with the black kids, which continued to alienate me from the white kids. The way I saw it, the black kids had all the fun while the white kids acted stiff and stuffy. To top it off, I played a lot of sports, so most of my friends were black athletes.

I loved sports. In the fall I played football; in the winter I played basketball; and in the spring I ran track. I soon excelled. My first year in football, the coach didn't know what he had. I vividly recall the opening game of the season. We lacked enough uniforms for everyone on the team, so the coach made me wear a practice jersey during the game. I was so embarrassed! His message to me was obvious: you won't see a lot of playing time and you definitely won't be a starter. The reason I remember that game so well is that by the next week, I wore my own game jersey.

And I started.

I played defensive end in football and forward on the basketball team; I competed in the long jump, high jump, high hurdles, low hurdles, and the 400 meters on the track team. And I was really fast.

High school was a blend of athletics and academics, and I did well in both. As graduation neared, the principal asked me to give an inspirational speech at our commencement ceremony. Frenché Brewer, a black girl, was asked to give one as well. Even in 1975, there was a certain degree of political correctness: white male, black female, everyone is happy.

It was a complicated juxtaposition of emotions: I was accepted in high school because of my athletic ability: yet, I still felt alone on a human level. But I knew I wasn't completely alone because the Lord Jesus was my friend. No matter how the kids at school treated me, nothing could compare to what Christ went through for people just like me. He endured much more than I ever would.

But my commitment to Him would be tested and taken to the next level: I was off to college.

Dartmouth

I viewed my upcoming start in college as a blank canvas. I could be whatever I wanted to be. No one knew me. All was fresh.

During my senior year in high school, I had determined that I wanted to attend an Ivy League school. I applied to Yale, Dartmouth, and Brown and was accepted at the latter two, but Yale passed on me. I was drawn to Dartmouth, so I entered in the fall of 1975.

One of my brothers told me that God was not leading His children into the darkness of a liberal arts education at an Ivy League school. He believed God's plan included only Christian colleges; he reasoned that God wants us to study under professors who believe in Jesus. According to him I would not be in God's will by attending Dartmouth College. I hoped otherwise and stayed the course.

I was a decent student, but I excelled in athletics. Ivy League athletic programs were run without the aid of scholarships, so I simply showed up on the field for the first day of football practice. Even though I was blessed with speed, the day the coach timed our forty-yard dash I burst off the starting line only to fall down! Even with that fall, I clocked in at 4.8 seconds! They let me try again, and minus the fall, I ran a 4.5.

I became a safety on the freshmen football squad. We had a good team that year, and I thoroughly enjoyed playing. Nobody could beat us that season. It was heady stuff.

But perhaps the pivotal point for me personally occurred after the conclusion of our final game as a freshmen squad. We were on the road at Boston College, and we had just defeated them soundly. We celebrated our accomplishment of going undefeated for the season. After we showered and dressed, we boarded the buses heading back to Dartmouth. As was our normal routine, we stopped for a post-game dinner. We always chose steak, so we found a steak house along the highway, parked the bus, and piled into the restaurant's back room.

I was so excited about our season, yet I wanted to make some sort of statement regarding my spiritual life. Up to that point in college, I had failed to gain any spiritual traction, so I thought it might be as good a time as any to try.

So in the midst of all the whooping, hollering, and celebrating, I decided to stand and ask for everyone's attention for just a moment. The team respected me, so they complied. I cleared my throat and began my admonition: "Guys, I know we're excited about an undefeated season, but there's a word I want us all to remember." With that introduction, I proceeded to open my Bible to the book of Ecclesiastes and read aloud the following passage:

> Rejoice, young man, during your childhood, and let your heart be pleasant during the days of young manhood. And follow the impulses of your heart and the desires of your eyes. Yet know that God will bring you to judgment for all these things.
>
> So, remove vexation from your heart and put away pain from your body, because childhood and the prime of life are fleeting.
>
> Remember also your Creator in the days of your youth, before the evil days come and the years draw near when you will say, "I have no delight in them."
>
> —Ecclesiastes 11:9-12:1

The guys looked at me in stunned silence. I was not sure why I had decided to make this proclamation, other than the fact that I had been cruising on autopilot and those were the words that came out!

For the next couple of weeks I tried to make sense of what I wanted out of my spiritual life when another incident occurred, but this one was of a very different variety.

I was invited to a party on campus, and since I was always the shy one, I decided to go! I don't remember all of the details, but I do recall a particularly tasty "fruit punch" that a group of guys were serving from a high-class punch bowl—one of their trash cans! The beverage was known around campus as "green machines."

Before the night was over, I had enjoyed more of the fruit punch than I had ever enjoyed before, and as a result became absolutely blind stinking drunk. Somehow I got back to my dorm room, but the lingering memory of that evening was spending the rest of the night sleeping in the bathroom with my head in the toilet.

To make matters worse, I was headed home the next morning. During that bus ride from Dartmouth to Syracuse, I had a lot of time to think. First, I vowed to never get hammered like that again. *God, take away that desire, please,* I prayed. While I was praying, I also decided that it was time to get serious about my relationship with Him. *God, I know all about You, but that is not a relationship with You. I'd love to transform my life to a place where You talk to me, and I'd have a real Biblical connection with You.*

Looking back I can see that I desired to move from knowledge to experience. My goal was to move from knowing Christ as Savior to knowing Him as Lord.

I want this relationship with You to be so real, I continued my prayer, *that if Billy Graham, the Pope, and Mother Theresa all said God was fake, I'd still know that You are the genuine article.*

And God heard my prayer. He answered it. I felt as if the Lord was saying, *Dave, are you calling Me? You called; I'm coming. I will take care of you, my son.*

Thank God for answered prayers.

But they weren't answered right away. Autumn led to winter and it seemed to go that way spiritually as well. Despite all the earnest praying, the months that followed the end of the fall term were spiritually bleak and cold, just like the New England landscape.

The spring of 1976 brought hope and new life to my journey. At the beginning of the spring quarter, freshmen were allowed to rush for fraternity membership and, of course, I headed right to the football fraternity, Theta Delta Chi. I was accepted, and I looked forward to all the rights and privileges of being a Theta Delt.

The night of initiation the Lord sent such a strong message to my conscience that I couldn't shake it. *This is not what I want for you,* the voice spoke strongly to my spirit. And I knew it was true. I looked around and decided that I didn't want to belong to a fraternity after all. Sometime after midnight, I left the initiation.

The next day I swallowed hard, took a deep breath, and paid a visit to the rush chairman, who was the captain of the football team. "What happened to you, last night, Stone?" he inquired, curiosity in his voice.

"I've been doing a lot of thinking," I began, "and I've decided Theta Delt is not what I want."

"Really?" he replied with surprise.

"Really," I answered, my inner strength growing.

"So what are you telling me, Stone?"

"I am saying that I want to de-pledge."

The power of that statement just hung in the air for what seemed like hours. Finally, the captain replied, "Okay, if that's what you want, that's what we'll do. By the way, you're free to come around the house any time you want."

I was amazed at how powerful it was to take that stand. The captain could have chewed me up and spit me out, but for some unexplained reason, he chose to be kind and understanding. I am convinced it was God directing the entire scene.

I say that because I chose to focus on God more and more as the spring term unfolded. I became almost obsessed with this idea: how do I have a Bible story happen in my life as opposed to just reading about it?

Enter Dave Zelie.

The Dartmouth Area Christian Fellowship was an active charismatic fellowship in the area with Dave Zelie as one of its leaders. We became friends, one thing led to another, and before too long we had started an Athletes Bible Study on campus. I was thrilled because I finally had a venue where I could get serious about some of the issues I had concerning the reality of my spiritual life. Dave was a good leader and a great friend. The study was just what I needed.

Once a month, all the campus Bible study leaders met with Dave. We began each study with silent prayer. I had no problem with that part of the program, but the next part really threw me. "Now, let's go around the room," Dave instructed, "and share with one another what you heard in your prayer."

I was stunned. It was my first challenge to hear the voice of God in a personal way. *What we heard in our prayers?* I repeated the phrase over and over in my mind. Initially it was too much. What did I hear in my prayer? My honest answer would have to be a big, "Nothing!"

"Well, I have to leave now," I suddenly announced to the rest of the group. "I have a mountain of laundry that I need to tackle, plus I have three tests tomorrow so I gotta study." And with those lame excuses, I was out of the room.

But Dave Zelie didn't give up on me. No, with Dave it was just the opposite. He invited me to spend time with him one-on-

one. I could ask him any and all questions that plagued me about my spiritual life. As I listened to his answers, they made sense. All the information he gave was coupled with the fact that he lived what he taught. In the language of the New Testament, Dave Zelie discipled me, and I ate it up like a starving man at an all-you-can-eat buffet.

Eventually Dave asked, "Have you ever been baptized?"

"As a kid, yes, but not as an adult," I replied.

"I see," he answered.

"Should I?" I inquired.

"Well, the Bible tells us about events that you might want to get aligned with and baptism is one of them."

So I got baptized. But it didn't happen in a church with a beautiful baptistery constructed specifically to celebrate such a special occasion. No, the way I saw it, baptism is telling the world on the outside about what is happening spiritually to you on the inside. So my baptism wasn't confined to a church.

I got baptized in the swimming pool on the Dartmouth campus.

It truly was a wonderful occasion, but it didn't stop there. Dave continued to disciple me, and he began preparing me to lead a Bible study on my own. Those times of preparation were rich times indeed. I remember fondly those early days of learning how to listen to the voice of God through my mind, my heart, and my circumstances. I needed to create action in my spiritual life and fully embrace all this good stuff for which I was clamoring.

When the spring term concluded, I decided I wanted to be closer to my girlfriend, Trina. So I spent the summer in Sumter working on her dad's farm. It was demanding physical work—mending fences, baling hay, tending to the cows. But it was worth it because I was close to my sweetheart—sort of. My sweetheart took a summer job in Myrtle Beach, South Carolina, which was two hours away! So the whole reason I went home was still hours away from me, but at least I got to know her brother better.

Returning to Dartmouth for my sophomore year brought some exciting changes. First of all, I became one of only a few sophomores chosen to play on the varsity football team. And then I became one of only a couple of sophomores to start, which was an accomplishment. But before I start to sound like a braggart, let's put it in perspective. Those were not powerhouse years for the Dartmouth squad. Our team's major goal was to win the Ivy League Championship. We did not win it for four straight years: 1974–1977.

So football was fun, exciting, and challenging, but I was wrapping my mind around a new area of interest academically. I entered Dartmouth my freshman year as a premed chemistry major in hopes of pursuing a medical career like my father. But the good Lord had other plans for me; that freshman year of academics didn't go well. So I changed my major, and it turned out to be a wise decision.

I became a math major my sophomore year and found a class I loved. As a matter of fact, it was my first A at Dartmouth.

It was computer science.

I enjoyed the class, and the subject matter came easily to me. Professor Fred Harris taught most of the computer science classes, and he became a favorite teacher of mine. In the spring of my sophomore year, I took one of his classes. It included an assignment to write our own programming language. The Programming Language (TPL) was taught over a ten-week time frame. Each week of class the language grew, which allowed the user more and more capabilities. The professor gave each of us the assignment, which we showed him every Friday. His job was to break the code of every student. I gained notoriety immediately by giving my TPL the name PTL, which I thought was a combination of cute, funny, and a strong Christian testimony. Nobody laughed.

About seven weeks into the course, we got into the topic of recursion—the idea that a language has to have a function and it has to be able to handle itself. It can be challenging, but I grasped the concept and wrote a module that was short, yet met the requirements. I showed up for a one-on-one meeting on Friday ready for Dr. Harris to review what I'd come up with.

His initial evaluation was less than positive. "Mr. Stone, what you've done is too short to handle what I have asked you to do." Then he added with almost-fiendish glee, "I am going to break it!"

And so he went for it. What he thought would be a simple task proved to be exceedingly difficult. He struggled, and as much as he tried to hide it, the strain became apparent. His body language gave him away. He started the task in a relaxed manner, but before too long he was leaning in, every muscle tensed. He gave it his best shot, but apparently his initial observation was incorrect. I did it.

Finally, in complete and utter exasperation, Professor Harris pushed himself away from the desk. He collected his composure, turned my way, and made the following pronouncement: "Dave, that is the most robust and elegant code I have ever seen for this requirement."

I let those words swim around in my head. I came away from that class with a strong message. What I heard from the professor was: *You have a gift.* I felt like I had discovered a God-given talent other than my athletic ability. Basically, a professor in a math class at a liberal arts college in the Ivy League was part of God speaking to me.

Dartmouth College gave me a fresh start. It was a place where God was growing in me through all aspects of college life: academics, athletics, Greek life, and church.

Changes in Focus

After my sophomore year, I once again planned to spend the summer in Sumter with Trina. My parents, however, had other plans, and I was invited to spend the break with them in Upstate New York. I went home to their cottage at Henderson Harbor on Eastern Lake Ontario, a brutally nice locale in the summer.

I did manage to get Trina to visit, and her time with us included a camping trip with my parents. I figured I could lose them somewhere in the Adirondack Mountains so I could have a little time alone with my beautiful girlfriend. God, however, had different plans and brought rain upon us like we were the family of Noah. Rather than time alone with my sweetie, the trip is best encapsulated by the mental picture of the four of us all trying to sleep in the same tent— Trina on one side of my father and mother, and me on the other. Incredibly romantic, yes?

It was during that summer that another event, seemingly insignificant, occurred and forced me to take a long, hard look at who and what I was becoming. Our family, like many, had their share of pets. We had the cutest Shetland sheepdog named Jock. He brought hours of love and joy to our family, and it goes without saying, our affections ran deeply for him. That summer Jock was chasing a ball, ran out in the street to retrieve it, and was run over by a car. We rushed Jock to a veterinarian who examined him and reported that our precious dog had a ruptured diaphragm, and the doctor couldn't save him. With great sadness and reluctance, we agreed to have the vet put Jock down. It led to one of my saddest moments, standing next to Dad as we silently buried Jock's broken body in our backyard. The silence was only interrupted by the sounds of us crying like babies.

I couldn't shake it. My parents owned a thirty-two-foot sailboat with a little dinghy behind it. I remember rowing that dinghy out into the harbor and crying so hard my whole body shook. Upon reflection, I believe I was trying to sort out my own emotional state brought on by losing our dog.

I began to ask myself important questions. What is life? What are my dreams? What is my future? At the time I hoped for a future as a professional football player or perhaps an Olympic decathlete. It occurred to me out in the harbor that my life was all about taking a game to the next level as opposed to taking life to the next level.

Jock's death rattled me. Who I was, what I based my identity on—that one event aroused many questions. I made some decisions. I decided to focus more on what was going on inside rather than what was going on outside. I was serious about it. In my quest to concentrate more on internals over externals, I made some immediate external changes. Up to that point in my collegiate life, I had taken pride in sporting a massive crop of long, flowing blond hair. I liked the way you could see it from the back of my football helmet during the games; it looked cool and I knew it contributed to my big man on campus persona. I felt like Sampson of the seventies.

But that day, when I got the dinghy back to shore, I just knew God was speaking to me. His message was brief but clear. You think you're handsome with your long, blond hair and athletic body. That's not as important to me. I want to develop your inner man.

I returned to Dartmouth for football preseason camp wondering about my inner man. After two-a-day practices, I would rest in my dorm room with two teammates who were also my roommates, Dave Brown and Curtiss Rooks. We discussed girlfriends, football, and God, usually in that order. After a few days of camp, they knew I was searching for something. I tried my best to explain how I wanted to focus on my inner man.

I began looking for Bible stories to help me. I found one about Jesse showing off his good-looking sons to Samuel, who was looking for the next king. God told the prophet, "Man looks on the outward appearance, but the Lord looks at the heart." Another one was Absalom. He knew he was attractive, so he would cut some of his beautiful hair and sell it. I thought pretty highly of my looks, and my hair was an important part of my identity.

I felt like I was supposed to get rid of my hair! Late one night during preseason camp, after the three of us finished talking, I went into our bathroom. Using a pair of scissors and a razor, I cut off my hair and shaved my head. When I stepped out, both of my roommates were shocked. I looked pretty funny with a tanned face and bleach-white, bald head. Shortly after that Curtiss joined the bald club.

Dave was not about to shave his head though. First, we looked goofy. Second, he was already losing his hair naturally. In some ways, cutting our hair was a little thing, but to the two of us it represented the release of a strong, external symbol.

It all sounded so spiritual. It all sounded so right. It all sounded so positive. But my newly discovered focus was not without its difficulties. I encountered a major problem right away that fall—on the football field. The coaches read my new internal focus as a loss of concentration athletically, and they took away my role as a starter. During my junior year, it was painful to be second-string and bald. I would have preferred to be a starter and bald. Following God didn't give me the success I desired that fall. But that's the way it panned out.

It was another trying year for the football team, the fourth year that we didn't win the championship. We were above .500, but that's about all we could say. Our head coach resigned at the end of the season. I imagined that what they viewed as my "loss of focus" didn't help the situation at all.

My loss of focus was apparent in my other sport, track, as well. I participated in winter track that year, but could see clearly that I was not progressing. I wanted to go to the Olympics as a decathlete, but it wasn't going to happen for an athlete who was described as simply "okay." I needed to excel. Once I realized the unlikelihood of a future in track, I finished up the winter season but opted not to join the team for spring. It was a monumental change for me.

That spring I decided to get on with my life, including pushing myself even harder academically. Even though I changed my major to economics, I did some simple calculations and discovered that I could graduate early. Instead of graduating the following June, I realized I could graduate in December if I really applied myself. I felt exhilarated by the thought of getting out of school six months early and avoiding another winter in Hanover. There were certain aspects of economics that overlapped the math I had studied, so the quantitative economics came naturally to me.

In the summer of 1978, I took a class entitled "The History of Economic Thought" taught by a young Muslim from East Pakistan named Salim Rashid. I found the subject matter fascinating, but it was one assignment in particular that completely caught my focus. We were required to complete an extensive research project on one major economist. As I discussed options with the professor, he made a suggestion that blew my mind. "Why don't you research John Wesley?" he asked.

"The preacher?" I replied.

"Yes, that's correct," he nodded. "Wesley's influence on England and its economic well-being kept the French Revolution from jumping the English Channel over to England. Without his attention, the English commoners would have come unglued."

As he smiled at me, I knew what was going on. Salim Rashid was aware I was a Christian, and he was trying to put something together for me that would have value beyond researching an economist. So I agreed to study John Wesley and thanked the professor for his helpful guidance.

One of the best parts of my research that summer was taking the time to read all of John Wesley's journals, which was an ambitious project. I learned about his philosophy of economics—how he required every person to bring something (usually money) to each meeting he held in order to assist those in need. I also discovered John Wesley coined the phrase "cleanliness is next to godliness;" it didn't come from the Bible.

As I read through the journals, I also saw my own spiritual journey mirrored in the life of this great man. Methodism was growing, Wesley was known for his disciplined life, but something supernatural occurred in the midst of this context ... Wesley was born again!

"I was leading people to Christ while I was going to Hell," he wrote. Through the kind direction of the Moravians, Wesley was encouraged to develop a personal relationship with God through Jesus Christ. Salvation is by grace, not by works. He began reading Martin Luther's *Introduction to Romans*, and that was all it took. John Wesley was truly born again. Similarly, his brother Charles followed the same pattern. Charles became very sick but was born again, and he was healed.

The mirror was so accurate. Previous to his conversion, John Wesley believed, but no differently than the Devil believes. Just like I did. But when he was truly born again, his life was never the same. I was excited by what I read. It was an affirmation from the Lord regarding His hand on my life.

So the professor got his research paper. I wrote about how John Wesley and the Christians of England built a social system to help the down-and-out people survive. It was a good economics paper. But to me, it was so much more.

The Lord continued to direct me. The next big step happened later that summer. The Dartmouth Area Christian Fellowship sponsored an event on campus in August that marked me for the rest of my life. The focus of the meeting was on spreading the Gospel of God's love around the world, but they were targeting a specific part of the world. The speaker called it the "10/40 Window."

"Most of the people who don't know Jesus Christ as their personal Savior live ten degrees north to forty degrees north of the equator," he explained. "This would include North Africa, the Middle East, India, Central Asia, and East Asia."

The speaker continued by explaining about the organization he represented. It's called Youth with a Mission, or YWAM for short. The agency exists for the purpose of releasing young people into missions. The more I heard about YWAM, the more excited I became. "So, I encourage all of you to get involved with missions in some manner," he implored. "And for some of you, there are a couple of steps you can take. You may want to investigate missions at the U.S. Center for World Missions in Pasadena, California. You may want to continue your studies there in either undergraduate or graduate work. Or you can join YWAM for study and short-term mission trips."

This man's words deeply impacted me. Missions involve every Christian, not just the ones called to be missionaries. Some will go, but the rest of us play many roles supporting those that go. I needed to find my role. He also mentioned that business people had a unique opportunity to impact countries in the 10/40 Window. Some countries would not tolerate card-carrying missionaries. However, business was welcomed everywhere. Perhaps I had studied at Dartmouth in order to create a business career that could be what God used to open doors to foreign countries. It's the ministry of the Gospel through business!

The day after that event, some of us who attended the meeting got together for a prolonged prayer. We had been so moved by the content of the message that we needed some spiritual perspective about how to take it all in. As we prayed I felt the Lord talking directly to me. I had come a long way from the days of being uncomfortable in listening for the voice of God in my prayers. I delighted in the sound of His voice. So there we were in the middle of a group of collegians engaged in a season of prayer. And God speaks. To me.

David, Afghanistan is the country for you.

I heard God's voice with unmistakable clarity. Right after I heard Afghanistan, I realized the next step for me was the U.S. Center for World Missions. It only made sense. Trina was also at that event and the prayer meeting. We were serious as a couple, and it was affirming to know what I felt from the Lord was being replicated in her life as well. We were in sync.

Those events changed the trajectory of my life during the final fall semester of my college career. I applied to the Center for World Missions and was accepted. In my acceptance package, they included a movie I used to raise financial support for the purpose of going to this school. I didn't know how God was going to provide the money for me to go to Pasadena, but I just knew He wanted me to go in preparation for work in missions and eventually to Afghanistan.

When I shared my new plans with my parents, I had no idea how they would respond. This would all be new information for them, and I could imagine their reaction going in a variety of directions. So suppose my indescribable joy when my mom and dad heard my plans and replied, "We would like to cover the costs completely." It was an overwhelming affirmation of God's unmistakable direction in my life. I could not have been happier. It was all coming together; the Lord was going to prepare me in an endeavor that would have an impact on the 10/40 Window!

That fall quarter of my senior year was wonderful. I was clear on the big picture of my life: heading to Pasadena and ultimately on my way to Afghanistan. Even our football team rallied after all those years of frustration! Under our new head coach, we went six and three and won the Ivy League Championship. By then I was no longer starting every game, but I enjoyed the season immensely.

And it was a stimulating time for me spiritually. I was still helping lead the athlete's Bible study on campus, which had evolved to a study primarily for guys from the football and basketball teams. I zeroed in on memorizing Bible verses that autumn. I carried around my three by five index cards, learning by heart as many verses as I could. I owned a King James Version Open Bible (the one with the blue cover) and studied it with a newfound fervency.

Academically I fulfilled my goal of finishing early, concluding my education at Dartmouth in December of 1978. I went back to New York to stay with Mom and Dad for Christmas. Then it was off to South Carolina to visit with Trina and her family before going to Pasadena where I was located early in January of 1979. Then the bottom dropped out of my life's plan. It came in the form of a letter from my parents.

Dear David:

We have been thinking a great deal about your future plans and we have decided that studying in Pasadena is not the right next step for you. We think getting a job is what you need to do next. Therefore, we have decided we are not going to support you financially in Pasadena. Stay in South Carolina and get a job so you can be near Trina or come back up here. We just don't want you to go out to California.

Love,

Mom and Dad

I've had years to reflect on their decision. In their defense my parents were far from anti-missions. Their view was that missions were everywhere. There were people in need in every country. They felt I could stay in the United States and be an effective worker for God—I didn't need to go halfway around the world to accomplish that objective. I'm sure they must have considered the financial resources they had contributed to my Dartmouth education. Do something here with the education you already have! All of those issues were reflected in their letter.

In further defense of my parents, in 1991, twelve years after that letter, my mom and dad felt the call to the foreign mission field and spent two years in Africa as medical missionaries! They sold their home and nearly everything they owned in order to free themselves for that assignment. "We're going over there for two years unless we die there!" my father said to me. No one else in our family has ever demonstrated that sort of commitment before. I am so proud of my parents.

But back in 1979, all I knew was my dream had been shattered. There was no way to raise support in such a short period of time, and I was officially broke. There was nothing left to do but get a job. I decided to start my career in South Carolina so at least I could be close to Trina.

Trina

For the record, I fell in love with her first.

She was pretty and intelligent; she loved the church scene and the athletic scene; she was well-respected by her peers, and I just knew it was God's will for the two of us to be together forever.

She was a wonderful combination of formality and polish with a fun-loving side that was so endearing.

And for the record, this girl could kiss.

There are many ways to look at the union between a man and a woman. But for me, if she can't kiss, the deal is off. I thank the good Lord every day that when I was in the tenth grade and she was in the ninth, I kissed Trina and knew I had found the one.

I really liked her, but she didn't like me. Fortunately for me, we lived close to each other so I could hang around her house regularly. And God blessed me mightily with one more fine piece of ammunition … Trina's mom really liked me. So there were seasons in our young lives when we were less boyfriend and girlfriend and more like what people used to call kissing cousins.

We had every season you can imagine. I'd like her, but she wouldn't like me. She'd like me, but I decided I didn't like her. We even dated a couple of each other's friends—that was interesting.

But all in all, I wanted things to get more serious with this young woman named Trina Bruner.

My big break came during the summer between my junior and senior year in high school. Trina was in Brevard, North Carolina, attending a national student council convention. Since I spent so much time over at their house, I knew from listening to her mom that Trina needed a ride back from the convention. It was a bit of a commitment, since it was at least three hours away. Who would drive three hours up there and three hours back? "I'd be delighted to help you out, Mrs. Bruner," I politely volunteered. I don't know what Trina's mom was thinking, but she agreed to my offer.

Trina was surprised to see me as her driver at the end of the convention. She may have even been a little pleased herself with this development! I wanted this trip to be special. "You know how we like to go creek hiking?" I asked her after we had driven a short distance.

"Yes," she replied.

"Well, you know of all the spectacular creeks that are not too far from here. What do you say we take a little detour from our direct route home and head over to one of those creeks? Would you like that?"

"Yes, that sounds fine."

So we headed over to an area in North Carolina near her grandfather's mountain house. It was the perfect setting. For the first time in a long time, we were actually alone, just the two of us. No other friends, family, or parents. As we hiked the creek, I realized, *Wow, I could do this together for a long time!*

We sealed the deal by deciding to go steady.

That did it for me. My senior year in high school was officially dedicated to Trina. Everyone else was off the deck. She was my girl. That was also the year I injured my leg during football season. I was in a splint for six weeks, which was confining. Among the many normal routines of life I had to give up was driving. Trina signed on for chauffeur duty. This was working out well.

Especially since we had gone back and forth so much in the earlier years of our relationship. The Christmas before, for example, I wanted to give Trina a special present, but I wasn't sure how she would accept it. I wanted to give her a nice piece of jewelry. I had saved up my money, but I didn't know what to buy her. A few weeks before Christmas, I ran into Trina at a local jewelry store. I asked her to help pick out some jewelry—for another girl! She agreed to my request.

"What do you think Fran would really like?" I asked.

As Trina surveyed the store, her eyes fell upon a beautiful opal necklace. "Any girl would love this necklace," she replied.

"Great. I'll take it."

As December 25 approached, I knew if I handed Trina a present that looked anything like the jewelry box with the opal necklace in it, she wouldn't accept it. So I had to get creative. I found a box about the size of a small refrigerator, and I placed a brick in it alongside the jewelry box with the opal necklace. I wrapped it in festive holiday paper and gave Trina her Christmas present with no argument whatsoever.

"Wow, whatever it is, it's big and heavy," she exclaimed. Exactly what I wanted her to think. When she opened it and discovered the opal necklace; she was polite, but a bit uncomfortable. We were so up and down at that point that I couldn't blame her.

Incidents like that Christmas event made me appreciate going steady even more.

Besides spending six weeks in a splint, another big event in my senior year was applying to colleges for the upcoming fall. When I made the final decision in April to attend Dartmouth, my parents surprised me with an announcement of a decision of their own. "We're leaving South Carolina! We've decided to move back to Upstate New York; we'll be closer to you!"

I was stunned. All of a sudden it was "The Stones are leaving town," and I was left with dozens of questions. How was the move going to work? Most importantly, was I ever going to see Trina again? I was really upside down in my gut, but I knew I needed to trust God for the right outcome.

From Trina's perspective, it was a sad day that summer morning in 1975 when those two giant U-Haul trucks, filled to the top with all the Stone's personal belongings, headed north. I had told her repeatedly that I was committed to coming back to see her just as often as I could possibly do it. But she thought: *He's gone. And those two trucks hold everything that would hold him here. He's gone.*

Yet I knew differently. I could do it. I was committed to her. I had a great relationship with her parents. We just knew it would work.

I arrived on the Dartmouth campus in Hanover, New Hampshire, in the fall of 1975, ready and eager to learn. I quickly assessed the female population on campus and came to the conclusion that Dartmouth women were smart, but not my type. That would certainly help me in my commitment to Trina.

Homecoming weekend arrived that autumn and I invited Trina, her mother, and my mother to visit. It was Trina's first visit and I was psyched! I was already learning the Dartmouth terminology. They referred to girls like Trina as an HTH, which stood for Home Town Honey. Well, my HTH was impressed with the school, which was great news for me. When she returned home, she applied to Dartmouth for the following fall semester. She also applied to Columbia College in South Carolina, because her mom had gone there.

We were making it work my freshman year. We visited each other during every school break. I even surprised her by flying back for her high school graduation. I spent the summer of 1976 in South Carolina, making every effort I could to keep things going.

Things became complicated my sophomore year. Trina ended up staying in South Carolina, choosing to attend Columbia College. As I surveyed the incoming class of Dartmouth freshmen, I saw a girl named Kim who was cute, and she liked to ski. I started dating her. Not wanting to string Trina along, I wrote her a Dear John letter. This was the first stick in her eye, all compliments of David Stone.

But Trina didn't sit around moping about her life. No sir, she started dating other guys. The University of South Carolina offered many handsome prospects during the year I was "skiing" with Kim. It was a real time of power-hungry ego for me. I kept reminding myself how important I was. After all, I was a sophomore starting on the varsity football team. And mind you, this was a team that only played seniors! I was full of myself.

But as the year wore on, I realized what I fool I was. As school ended, I had already broken it off with Kim and decided I would spend the summer in New York with my parents. I visited South Carolina in order to win back Trina. She also made a trip to Henderson Harbor to visit me. In an act of gracious kindness, she took me back and I was more excited than ever.

I returned to Dartmouth for my junior year with a new thought on my mind: I was going to finish college as quickly as I could and then Trina and I were going to marry. I was taking heavy loads and had it all figured out. I could graduate in December of 1978, six months ahead of my classmates. Then I would graduate, move back to South Carolina, marry Trina, and all would be right with the world. I even started seeing more in my Bible readings that assured me that marrying Trina was God's plan for me. I had no doubts.

But Trina did.

She was not nearly as excited as I was about my upcoming plans. I tried my best to overlook her concerns, but this issue became the beginning of a large disconnect in relationship.

I stayed in Hanover for summer school since I was still on the program to graduate early. Trina came up to Dartmouth for summer classes. I had one message on my mind: "Get married—go, go, go!" Trina replied with her message: "Wait, wait, wait!" Her shopping cart was not yet at the checkout counter, whereas my stuff was already bagged.

"Let's pretend that we're just starting over again," she suggested. "Do you remember those days? Where it was a big step just to hold hands?"

The gap was widening.

At least we agreed that it would be good if we both concentrated on finishing college. I finished in December of 1978 and stayed in South Carolina after my plan to attend graduate school in California fell through. My first job was as a management trainee with Bankers Trust of South Carolina. After the training, I became the assistant branch manager and then an investment officer selling government bonds. I did that for a year and then Equitable Life Insurance Company hired me to sell life insurance.

Meanwhile Trina graduated from college and briefly entertained the thought of going on to medical school like her father. She decided against it and instead took a job in pharmaceutical sales.

By the end of 1980, I made another big decision. I decided to take a job that required me to move to Atlanta, Georgia. But I had my reasons. The job would allow me to save money for an engagement ring! The geographic distance didn't help us, but I knew everything would work out.

In January of 1981, I was back in South Carolina visiting, and I decided to keep things moving. Even though I didn't have the ring, I needed to make some progress. I took Dr. Bruner aside and asked for his daughter's hand in marriage. He said yes.

Fueled by his positive response, I decided to pop the question to Trina. She wanted to take things slowly, but I was pushing, pushing, pushing. I proposed to her without a ring! What was I thinking?

Well, whatever I was thinking, I was wrong. Trina did say, "yes," but the engagement didn't have the great feeling that accompanies a "yes." It didn't help matters that I was pretty clueless about the whole concept of romancing a woman. I replaced romance with a steady, relentless pounding of spiritual stuff that was awful. If I read a good book, I sent it to her. If I heard a good sermon, I gave her an audio copy of it. I projected onto her everything I thought would help her. And it was wearing her out. Our relationship limped along through the first few months of 1981 until Mother's Day.

That was the day Trina told me it was over.

Not only was it over, but Trina had another piece of commentary about the way I was spiritually bullying her:

"Dave, you are not my Holy Spirit!"

I was crushed.

She had a wonderful group of supportive friends who helped her through the transition. Before long she met another guy and they began dating. Her friends helped her see the contrast between the new guy and me. "Dave is not romancing you. He thinks it's a done deal. He thinks you should be engaged and he hasn't even given you a ring! Look at how attentive this new guy is. He is romantic, Dave's not."

Trina did wrestle with the decision however, and she talked it over with her dad one night.

"Dad, I think I got cold feet with Dave." He said he understood and his counsel was simple: "Follow your feet, sweetheart."

Like I said, I was crushed, but I picked myself up and got on with my life. I began dating a woman in Atlanta who worked at the Baptist Mission Board. She was very nice and we got along well. One night we were talking about our future when she said the strangest thing to me. "Dave, I really am fond of you. And frankly, you could be the one. But I still feel Trina around here. Do you have that feeling?"

I nodded in agreement.

"Well then, I think you need to get rid of it or go after it."

And that's when I picked up the phone and called Trina after a six-month hiatus. We chatted for a bit and then I told her how well everything was going with the woman I was dating.

"Is it serious?" Trina asked.

"Well, it could be," I replied, trying to be honest, not coy.

"I see," she said quietly.

I swallowed hard, took a deep breath, and said what I really wanted to say. "It could go into serious mode, but I only want that to happen if you tell me that we're really six feet under."

There was a pause that seemed like a millennium, but finally Trina replied. "Well, Dave, if you don't say the "M" word, I'd really love to see you again."

That's all I needed to hear. I immediately invited her to Atlanta for a visit. She accepted and came down for a weekend.

I discovered she could still kiss.

I spent that Christmas at her house and it quickly began to feel like things were getting back to normal. The first half of 1982 looked favorable for us. I promised her I wouldn't bring up marriage because I had a plan for doing it right the second time. It was all centered on her birthday.

On June 9, we drove to her brother's place to help with some of his chores. He had been in an accident and consequently was on crutches and needed some help around the house. Even though it was her birthday, I knew she would focus on helping Steve clean his house and then she would fix us supper. We would have cake and ice cream to celebrate her special day.

After dessert her brother, Steve, handed her a birthday gift, which I had hoped would happen. "Well, I have some gifts for you as well," I announced. And with that I brought in a pyramid of perfectly wrapped presents. On top was a very small box. I had Trina begin with the largest box so she would end with the smallest one. I had arranged each gift to progressively move toward the idea of marriage. With each gift Trina opened, Steve began looking for an excuse to find his crutches and leave us alone.

Trina was nervous and blurted out, "No, I think I'd like it better if you stayed!"

So I gave Trina her presents one by one. Granted, Steve was on the right track. Each gift had a connection to weddings or marriage. By the time we got to the last two gifts, Trina was beginning to break out into a cold sweat. The next to the last gift was a book entitled *How To Plan Your Wedding*. I smiled. Steve's face reddened. Trina laughed nervously. One tiny box was left—the kind of box that looked like it would hold a ring.

"I don't want to open this one," Trina confessed.

"It's okay," I reassured. "Don't worry about it."

She reluctantly opened the box to discover a beautiful pair of pearl earrings. Trina let out the biggest sigh of relief.

"I was so afraid that you were going to ask me to marry you," she admitted.

"Well, since you brought it up," I responded, to her surprise. And I got down on one knee in front of her.

"What's going on?" she asked.

"Trina, will you marry me?" With that heartfelt question, I reached into the pocket of my jeans and pulled out a diamond engagement ring.

"Yes," she whispered.

And all the angels in heaven rejoiced. Steve just sat and smiled, unable to move without his crutches.

On October 30, 1982, Trina Bruner became Mrs. David Stone. Her hometown was delighted with the outcome. After all, they had observed the half-hearted first engagement—the one without the ring and without the girl.

I have learned a great deal about marriage. It's not the idyllic image of two playful dolphins swimming in sync through the clear blue waters of an ocean. No, we rarely surface and dive at the same time. We don't swim in unison. We are on two different frequencies, but I have discovered our differences light up our lives. There is great truth in the axiom that opposites attract. The key is keeping that 'opposites attract' energy working in your behalf. Many couples miss out by growing weary of the differences. I have learned it can be exactly the opposite!

I am an intuitive and trusting person. Trina is more analytical; therefore, she takes longer to trust people. She is my quality control. Rarely is she wrong. In our business she balances out my enthusiasm with her cautiousness. She is compliant. I am not. If the speed limit is fifty-five miles per hour, I'll push it to sixty-three, and she will drive fifty-four.

She is an introvert. I am an extrovert. I am an optimist. I have often referred to Trina as a pessimist, but she quickly corrects me, "No, David, I am a realist." And she is completely correct.

Any woman who can stay with a man who is tough to handle is one strong woman.

I, David Stone, would qualify as a man who is tough to handle.

And Trina Stone would qualify as one strong woman.

And I love her more and more each day.

Benny Hinn

When the possibility for Pasadena passed me by after graduation from Dartmouth, I ended up back in South Carolina. I was gainfully employed at the Bankers Trust of South Carolina in Columbia. I became an active member at the Central Assembly of God in downtown Columbia. Best of all, I was near Trina. I was so poor I couldn't even afford a car—I walked everywhere or rode the bus. But I had a job, a church, and a girlfriend. I counted my blessings.

It was 1979. The Central Assembly of God scheduled a series of revival meetings featuring the famous TV preacher Benny Hinn. In preparation for the meetings, they asked church members to volunteer. Because I was a big guy, some of the folks at the church thought I would be good as one of Benny's helpers—with a specific task.

A typical Benny Hinn meeting included congregational worship with Benny singing (he's a terrible singer!), and then he would preach a sermon. Following the homily, he would begin the healing service. Many of the people Benny healed were "slain in the Spirit" during the healing process, and many of them would fall to the floor in an uncontrolled state. That's where I came in. I was enlisted as one of Benny's "catchers." I was there to catch anyone who fell so they wouldn't hurt themselves.

I was dutifully manning my position as a catcher for the healing part of the service. All was going according to the plan. However, I was totally caught off guard by what happened next.

I was standing behind the people waiting to be healed as Benny made his way toward them. At that point he stopped and looked past those people and stared right at me!

"I have a word from the Lord for you," Benny exclaimed as he looked straight at me. "God has His hand on your life."

He smiled at me and then went back to those waiting to be healed.

I didn't know what to make of it, but I never forgot it.

Even more amazing, Benny Hinn came into my life again in 1982.

I remained in Columbia through the end of 1979, and then I moved to Atlanta in 1980. Once I settled in, I found a wonderful church home at the Faith Memorial Assembly of God. Life proceeded as normal. Then in 1982 the church announced their upcoming series of revival meetings. The preacher for the event was Benny Hinn.

That time I was not one of the catchers. I wasn't even one of the volunteers. I sat in the congregation the night Benny Hinn preached. He was no more than five minutes into his message when he suddenly stopped. Why? Because he saw me.

"I gave you a word from the Lord some time ago," Benny said, looking right into my eyes.

All I could do was nod.

"He has given it to me again," he continued. "God has His hand on your life."

I was stunned. A word from the Lord twice? From the same guy? In two different cities?

I didn't know what to make of it beyond the fact that I had better listen up because the Lord Himself was trying to speak to me. More than ever, I began paying attention to my life. What did the messages mean? Ministry? If so, where? Here in the United States? In my career? How about foreign countries? Afghanistan?

It was almost too much to take in, but I kept these musings alive in my heart and continued to ask God for answers.

The Young Businessman

To say I moved around a bit in the job market is an understatement.

In the five years after I graduated from college, I had six different jobs!

Job number one was at Bankers Trust of South Carolina in Columbia. Transitioning from student to employee required some adjustments, including choice of attire. For most of my collegiate career, I wore corduroy pants (my favorites were light blue) with a tan sport coat over a collared shirt, finished off with a fine-looking pair of cordovan penny loafers. Showing up for the Management Training Program in this get-up brought a fair share of disapproving stares. The banker's uniform consisted of a white shirt, necktie, and business suit—the more conservative, the better. Having virtually no money presented a challenge until I discovered a treasure trove of fine clothing at … Goodwill.

Hart Schaffner Marx and Hickey Freeman suits hung side-by-side. And they were only five dollars a suit! I remember buying five or six of them. The coat fit; I just needed to get the pants tailored. That store saved me a bunch of money—enough to buy a pair of wing tip shoes to replace my penny loafers.

It worked out that the Management Training Program was six months long, because after six months it was unmistakably clear that I didn't want to be an assistant bank manager. I set my sights on another part of the bank that I found intriguing—the investment division. So I transferred to investments and began job number two selling bonds.

It was a tumultuous time in our country's history in late 1979 and early 1980. The U.S. Embassy in Iran had been taken, complete with hostages. The economy was in the tank. The markets were unusually volatile, and folks were looking for a safe place to invest their money. With the exception of the United States Ice Hockey team defeating the Soviet Union team during the Olympic Winter Games held at Lake Placid ("Do you believe in miracles? YES!"), there wasn't much to cheer about.

I immediately fell in love with the investment business. It was the work I loved. The people, on the other hand, drove me nuts. I can sum up the investment world with two words: rude and crude. I tried my best to stay above all the monkey business, but it was an extremely uncomfortable environment for me. I still had my goal of business with ministry. I focused on mastering the world of business and ministry in America. In my mind the dream was still alive. I wanted to be successful enough in business that I could fund my own short-term outreach experiences without financial assistance. No doubt, I wanted to make a lot of money, but the ultimate goal was the "being a witness" piece of the pie.

Then I realized that I was not going to get rich working at the bank. I needed to become one of those people the bank works for! They are the ones who are really rich. One of these men was in the insurance industry; he offered certified financial planning services too. It looked like an attractive avenue to make good money, plus have flexible hours—the total package. The more I looked into it, the more I liked what I saw, which led me to resign from my position at Banker's Trust in the spring of 1980 and accept job number three.

I started selling insurance for the Equitable. I had great expectations and high hopes. They were quickly dashed. I don't know what I was thinking; it didn't take me long to conclude that this wonderful opportunity to sell people all sorts of insurance sucked. Maybe not for everyone, but definitely for me.

The typical week began each Monday morning with a list of one hundred prospects for cold calls. I went to a couple of specific places to find my prospects. I went after anyone who had purchased a house or had children. I was looking for those thirty-something neighborhoods of the young and affluent. I could expect ten appointments from those one hundred calls. And I could expect one sale out of those ten appointments. It was hard work, but that wasn't my complaint. The problem with the insurance business was that once I was in it, everyone I knew became a prospect. Family, friends, neighbors, and mere acquaintances all became people who needed the essential services our insurance company provided. It just didn't feel comfortable to me.

I had only been at the Equitable a few weeks when I went to see my boss in mid-July. "I need a break," I told him. He graciously allowed me to take some time off, and I visited my Mom and Dad in

Upstate New York. It ended up being a perfect time to visit them, especially if you enjoyed hanging out with a bunch of beautiful women.

My folks were active volunteers in the Miss New York Beauty Pageant; the winner went on to compete for Miss America. The New York pageant was in high gear when I visited, so I attended all sorts of gala events while I was there. By the end of the week, I was unmistakably clear on the fact that I didn't want to sell insurance. I thanked Mom and Dad, went back to South Carolina, and resigned.

"Dear Lord, what is it that You want me to do next?" I prayed humbly and fervently. With no clear immediate answer, I found job number four at Trina's family farm. Gone were the days of the Hickey Freeman suits with the new wing tip shoes. It was manual labor, hard physical work. I didn't mind. My body was in good shape and the farming gave me the opportunity to look for what God wanted me to do next. When I wasn't working on the farm, I researched finance and computer programming careers.

As the fall of 1980 arrived, I found out about a job fair in Atlanta, Georgia. I attended and learned about a company out of Ann Arbor, Michigan, that was hiring people in Atlanta. Comshare was a computer time-sharing company. They had an entry level position available for a marketing consultant.

I took it.

I had to relocate to Atlanta. Not a problem for a young bachelor with few earthly possessions. I was in job number five by late autumn. This job was better for several reasons. First, I used my programming skills. Secondly, it put me in a variety of business environments. And thirdly, I enjoyed learning the marketing aspect of the business.

A typical client was Conoco Oil Company. They tracked every gas station's prices for all three grades of gasoline sold in each of their station's neighborhoods. By tracking the prices on our computers and with our software, they were able to price their gasoline lower than the competition, while still allowing them to make a profit.

The Equitable taught me about selling, but Comshare went further. I learned how to make executive presentations, business-to-business, thanks to the Dale Carnegie courses that Comshare required me to take. I also learned how to make technical presentations. "Here's what you imagine the computer doing. Now here's what it can actually do. And here's how we can make it happen!" I am so grateful for the value of learning these skills, because I still use them to this day.

The longer I was at Comshare, the bolder I became. For example, I have always thought that the book of Proverbs in the Old Testament is filled with wisdom for success in the marketplace. One of my favorite verses, from a rather obscure translation, hangs on my office wall.

Be timid in business and come to beggary.
Be bold and make a fortune.

—Proverbs 11:16b (NEB)

I began integrating Proverbs into my business environment. I did not lose sight of my goal: share God's love through business here and eventually in Afghanistan. I was laying the foundation; the cement was setting up. I knew I was doing what God wanted me to do.

In early 1982, a regional manager from Comshare provided vocational testing. I jumped at the chance to learn more about my skill set and perhaps get a better handle on the question of where I was going in Comshare. I knew I didn't want to live in Ann Arbor, Michigan, but I really was enjoying the opportunity to serve other businesses with cutting-edge software.

When my results came in, the manager called me to his office. As we sat down, he asked me some important questions. "Dave, what is it that you really want in your future business endeavors? What are your goals?"

I thought about it for a moment and responded, "I want to be the president of a software company somewhere in the South by the time I am thirty-five."

As soon as I said it, I braced myself for the reply. It was a classic set-up for an answer full of derision and mockery. But he didn't do that. Instead, he responded with an honest and kind affirmation. "Well," he said, "if that's your goal, then we have a lot of work to do!"

I was about twenty-five years old at the time, and we both knew I had a ten-year window to make my goal a reality. We decided it was a good for me to remain on the technical side of the company. The salespeople sold the product, while the tech people figured out how to make it happen. But Comshare got their tech people onstage, in front of the clients. We weren't hidden in a backroom, making things happen for faceless people. No, we were encouraged to mingle with the folks we worked with, and in doing so, we learned a great deal about how to create the right product. Once again, this principle stayed with me. At First Rate, we work hard to make sure very few people are considered backstage employees. We are all out there, and that is highly unusual for a technical support vendor.

Although the work at Comshare was positive, the highlight of 1982 was my marriage to Trina in October.

In January of 1983, a headhunter in San Francisco contacted me about an opportunity at an investment software business in Dallas, Texas. "Dave, they are looking for a guy just like you," he gushed. "They will have a representative in Atlanta soon, and I think the two of you should meet." It was the exact type of business that interested me, so I agreed to meet with the folks in Atlanta. The meeting went well—well enough that I flew to Dallas in early February to meet with them on site. On February 15, 1983, I resigned from Comshare, and on March 1, I began my first day at National FSI. My job title was programmer for their investment performance system. Some of my peers at National FSI, which ultimately came to be known as FSI, saw me as a Dartmouth graduate doing a job far beneath my level of accomplishment. They saw it as a step backward for me, but I was more than willing to do it because I wanted to learn this business from the ground floor up.

Of course, leaving Georgia was not easy—especially for Trina's family. Her mother was especially unhappy that I was moving her daughter west of the Mississippi. "When are you coming back home?" she would ask every time we spoke on the phone. I offered Trina the following plan: "Let's live in Dallas for five years, then we'll move to some place in California like San Diego for another five years. After we get all that out of our system, we'll move back East to Charlotte or Atlanta or Charleston in order to be close to the family." Trina was agreeable to the plan. As for me, five years anywhere sounded huge since I had never stayed in one place for longer than four years!

As noble as starting from the ground floor sounded, the notion was immediately tested. A friend of mine went to work for a young company called Lotus. Their 1-2-3 was taking the world by storm, so when my friend called a few weeks after my move to Texas and asked if I'd be interested in opening a Lotus 1-2-3 office in Dallas, I was sorely tempted, but I passed on the opportunity. Ironically, an insurance company in Georgia also approached me during that time; they guaranteed I would make a lot of money. A million dollars a month wouldn't be enough money to get me back into selling insurance!

My boss at FSI began teaching me everything I needed to know about the investment application business. I had a big learning curve, but I mastered programming, revenue responsibility, expenses responsibility, the whole ball of wax. Plus, we were involved in selling the product!

I worked for FSI from 1983 through 1989. SEI purchased FSI in 1989, and the new owners chose to keep me on through the rest of the decade. Life was rolling along. Business appeared good. Family life appeared good. I was still committed to my goal of doing business as a means to ministry overseas. As the eighties came to a close, all seemed fine with the world.

Then came the nineties, and it all turned upside down.

Starting the Business

It was 1990.

I was working for SEI, living in Arlington, Texas, driving down the Tom Landry Freeway every day to and from work, dreaming of another locale—Wayne, Pennsylvania. I wanted to be transferred to that little town just outside of Philadelphia, in the area known as the Main Line, where the corporate headquarters of SEI was located. It was where we needed to go for me to keep moving up in the company. It was logical. It made good business sense. But the Lord had other ideas.

On a hot July day in 1990, I was driving off the Tom Landry Freeway onto the Collins Street Exit. I could see a panoramic view highlighting all of North Arlington. As I approached the end of the exit, I had a truly extraordinary experience.

This part of Arlington is where you will have a company that will be the best expression of Who I am.

It was a voice. But it was more than a voice. I could see Who was speaking. It was God. And He was on the hood of my car.

Believe me, a visual, audible encounter with God is not the stuff of a typical day. But this was no ordinary day. God Himself was directing me to start a business that would become First Rate.

The thought of a new, successful business, blessed by God was appealing at that point in our lives. We were having serious financial difficulties, and we were taking it one day at a time. Our house was for sale, and we were willing to take a loss on it because we needed to get out from the monthly payments that had become too big for us to handle. A co-worker offered us his run-down, three bedroom, one and a half bath rental house. It was in such bad shape that Trina wouldn't even go in to look at it. But we could live there rent-free if we paid for our utilities. The house was for sale, so we would have to move out if and when it sold. But it was the kindness of friends and our church family that allowed us to survive those difficult days.

Trina was pregnant with our fourth child. Pregnancy is difficult enough under normal circumstances, but with the wicked Texas summer heat, three little ones, and all the financial stress, it was almost unbearable. Finally, in August Trina delivered our son Joshua. But it was a stillbirth. How could that be? On top of all our other struggles in life, we had lost our little boy?

It was a time of deep testing in the Stone household. Experts estimate that 80 percent of marriages end in divorce when a child dies in the family. Trina and I didn't want to be one of those casualties, so we worked hard on our marriage. From that vantage point, it was a time of personal and relational growth.

As 1991 arrived, things grew increasingly more difficult at work. SEI sent clear signals that my role was not crucial to them in their future. Our part of the company in Texas was in trouble, so much so that it looked like they would shut down the product I was managing.

In February, I came up with a bold plan: I would offer to buy our group from SEI. To my delight, when I proposed the idea, they liked it. We continued to meet, and we hammered out the deal. Ironically each time we met the deal got smaller and smaller, but nonetheless, my excitement grew. After weeks of effort we had set the first Friday in April as the closing date. I was almost giddy with delight knowing that the plan had finally come together.

Yet when I walked into the office that morning to sign the papers, immediately I knew something wasn't right.

Instead of the executives who were supposed to meet with me, the director of human resources showed up in their place. And instead of celebrating the sale, I sat in stunned silence as the director said to me, "Dave, we're going to have to let you go."

How could that happen? I went home to tell Trina, heartsick and embarrassed by this ugly turn of events. "I guess we need to look at moving to some other city where we can get work," I suggested weakly.

"Is that what you really think we should do?" she asked.

"Well ..." I stammered, "actually, I had an experience last July that I never told you about, and I think you should hear it." I told her of God's message to me about a company in Arlington.

"I haven't felt comfortable thinking about moving away," she confessed. "And now with this new information you've shared with me, I think we should stay here."

It was such a relief to hear her say those words. Our two visions were in alignment, and we didn't know how it was going to happen, but we knew God was going to take care of us in every way.

Over the next couple of months, we put together all of the necessary paperwork to create our own company. On July 15, 1991, we signed the incorporation papers, officially declaring our company as First Rate. As much as I love that name, it actually wasn't my first choice. I wanted to call our company Summit, but we discovered someone had beaten us to the punch; so when we found the name First Rate was available, we grabbed it.

I started the business with all the energy and excitement I could muster. I just knew that our existing clients would be more than happy to move from SEI to First Rate—all I needed to do was make them aware of our new set up. As July led into August, I hit the road to visit all of our clients. August became September, September turned to October, and we had yet to sign a client.

We had no business, no money, no savings. Once again, our church family was literally meeting our physical needs by bringing us food to eat. To spare us the obvious humiliation, they would come to our door late at night. They'd leave the food, knock on the door, and run away before we could see them.

Trina's father graciously offered to loan us money. If he hadn't, I don't know how we would have made it. What an amazingly difficult time!

November was no better than the previous months. But in the midst of all the Christmas celebration, by the end of December we had actually gotten close to a sale. It was truly a Happy New Year when First Rate signed its first client, PNC Bank, and received its first check for $30,000 on January 1, 1992.

We believed that we had belonged to God, so we wanted to honor Him by giving back at least 10 percent of what He had given us. So as our first act with that $30,000, we wrote our local church a check for $3,000. The Lord has found favor with us, so we bless Him by thankfully giving back a portion of His bounty.

As 1992 progressed, so did First Rate. Initially, we worked from home, but by mid-year we were able to rent an office space in town. By October we hired our first employee, John Watkins. At year's end we were moving along quite well.

The lessons we learned in those early days have had such a strong influence on the way we run our company, even to this day. We still donate ten percent of our revenue. We still talk about God freely in our company. We've even hired a chaplain to help meet the spiritual needs of our employees and their families. And I continue to learn and grow on this journey of life.

At last count we have eighty full-time employees. They come from different backgrounds, faiths, and dreams. We're trying to equip one another in the relationship with their God. As one of our employees put it: "My time at First Rate was a great stop for me. It helped me with my relationship with my God. Thank you, First Rate."

The real satisfaction in this company comes from the personal relationships. I love the investment performance business. I love the software business. But the bottom line is that the people we interface with in our day-to-day lives are the most important aspect. I want this company to outlast me!

Non-Business Matters

If you gain the whole world but lose your own soul, what do you have?

It was around this time of my life when I began to realize that I had focused everything around my business. I felt I had to—it was the time to give it my all in order to make it survive. It was the time to give it legs.

Fortunately, I was also heavily involved in church and community work as well.

Unfortunately, it was a time of major stress at home.

Our first born, Allan, was strong-willed, just like me. I was unequipped and unprepared for the work of parenting. I brought my work stress home in the form of emotional outrage. If Al did something wrong, I wouldn't just spank him, I would wale on him. Trina saw what was going on, but I was clueless. I didn't know how to deal with the conflicts at work without bringing them home, and I didn't know how to parent well. Those two aspects of my life made a pair of very ugly twins. To this day I am so grateful that I had friends and family who could help me see where I was off base and help me gain perspective.

In late 1987 we had become involved as a family at a church called Grace Baptist Church. We needed a church that focused on young families, and this church filled the bill. I became close friends with one of the associate pastors, a kind man named Lonnie Hayter. This was not an anomaly, since I had befriended those in the pulpit for years. Back when I lived in Atlanta, I lived with an assistant pastor. I have two brothers who are pastors. A roommate at Dartmouth became an Episcopal priest. So I do have a propensity that draws me to these kinds of godly men.

Lonnie was more nontraditional than most pastors, which was something we found attractive. Unfortunately the rest of the church didn't see it that way, and by 1993 Lonnie was given his walking papers. Being his close friend, our family went with him. He started a church called New Beginnings, and the Stone family was proud to be part of his congregation.

Lonnie and I talked about developing a close relationship as far back as 1988. The conversation came up after we had learned that a big time pastor had tanked out morally. Lonnie and I talked about having a friendship that would endure bad news. "When something bad comes to light, will you run in or run out?" we asked each other.

"We're in," we replied, and we've been committed to each other ever since.

The early nineties was a time for getting people involved in church leadership who were not theologically trained. As New Beginnings took off, we realized that we didn't have enough money to hire a staff person to work with the youth. One day Lonnie came up to me and said, "Dave Stone, would you consider becoming our part-time youth pastor?"

"What does part-time mean?" I asked.

"Obviously you could continue to work your Monday through Friday job. We just need someone to run the Wednesday night youth meeting and the Sunday morning and evening sessions—and a few weekend activities—and we're talking for both junior and senior high."

And that's how I became the youth guy.

Needless to say, we employed lots of babysitters at that time in our lives.

In the midst of it all, I was discovering an important principle in my life. I could be an influencer in the life of young people who were dealing with issues with their own parents. I could be cool, entertaining, relevant, Christ-centered, and since I knew their parents, I could serve as a go-between.

I found great satisfaction working with youth, even though I still had issues with my own children.. To this day I am still drawn to young people. I am attracted by their enthusiasm. I am willing to listen to them and I find that listening is more important to them than any sort of magical message that I may embrace. It's the well-worn adage, "people don't care how much you know until they know how much you care." I wanted to be an adult the kids could talk to. I wanted them to know my vision was to reach youth and mobilize youth, because that's how to build a successful ministry. Youth groups work when the kids drive it, not the adults.

I was committed to making the Scriptures relevant. There is a way to accomplish learning the Word of God that isn't rigid and formal. And the kids related to it. My observations at the time centered on the fact that the church seemed very left-brained, or analytical, in its presentations, whereas kids absorbed more from a right-brained, or creative, approach to learning. I asked kids questions like, "What is the culturally appropriate expression in coming to Jesus?" And, "What will a person look like after they come to Him?" I was seeing kids come to faith who didn't always look cleaned up on the outside like most adults thought they should have looked. And that was all right with me.

I enjoyed my life as a part-time youth pastor, yet I continued to avoid the fact that my young family was struggling with financial issues and parenting issues. Lonnie eventually approached me with the question that brought it all to a head.

"Dave, you are doing such a great job as the part-time youth pastor, I would like you to consider going from part-time to full-time."

I was honored that he asked me, but I didn't take long to give him my answer. "I think I will be a better help to the church by staying in the business world rather than jumping out and going full-time with you."

Lonnie said he understood. I have always believed that people on fire for God need to have more options than just becoming a pastor. I can be equally, if not more, effective ministering from the world of business.

It was a wise decision, not only philosophically, but practically as well. The stress continued to escalate on the home front. I was still clueless, thinking I was doing the right things by building what a good husband, father, and business leader ought to be building. But things looked good onstage while they were very different backstage.

I was putting a lot of pressure on my kids, especially Al. As he grew up, he became more stubborn, which only made me equally hardheaded. *This strong-willed kid is going to be successful so that he won't embarrass me*, I found myself thinking. *He will get good grades and be well behaved so that I look good as an elder at the church, president of a service organization, and president of a company. It's that simple.* I had a reputation to uphold and I was determined to do it, no matter whom I hurt. I had too much at stake in all those other arenas. There was a reputation to uphold, even at church. After all, I was an elder, worship leader, had a young marrieds' Bible study in our home—I was a spiritual leader!

Disciplining the kids created the worst situations. Instead of a swat with a paddle, it was a whack. Trina demanded that it stop. So I would swat only once but the rest of the rage was still there. I remember promising Trina, "I will never yell at the kids again." And if I was lucky, that promise lasted for a week before I started again. I needed to learn to deal with my frustration from work, the source of my anger. The promise became, "I will express my anger at work so I don't need to yell at home."

It was the truth. Starting a new company guarantees a hefty load of stress. Four out of five businesses fail during the first five years; only 80 percent of the remaining businesses survive the second five years! We experienced normal growing pains—not the least of which was the constant stress of cash flow and making payroll. I was fortunate that I was able to hire really good men and women. They helped build a business that reflected the best of who I really was.

A true turning point in the business took place in January of 1993. I had developed deep relationships with three men whom I loved and respected. I invited the three of them to join me on a three-day off-site getaway to help me set some plans in motion for my business. My hope was that if I could get the company running more smoothly, I could be more accessible to my family. My friends—Lonnie Hayter, Tim McKibben, and Dan Linehan—accompanied me on what became an annual planning getaway. Tim was especially helpful in moving me toward an annual plan for 1993. Tim is a master at asking the hard questions with firmness surrounded by compassion.

"Do you have a budget for the year?" he asked.

"No," I answered honestly.

"Will you do one?"

"Yes."

"When?"

"By the end of January."

"How long will it take you to do it?"

"Two full days."

"What two days will you block out to do it?"

"January twentieth and twenty-first."

"So we can meet you on January twenty-second to review what you have created?"

"Yes."

Tim's accountability connection continued through the process.

"How much are you budgeting for your office space this year?" he asked.

"Five hundred dollars a month," I answered.

"Okay, I will hold you to it."

"Okay."

"So don't spend six hundred dollars a month."

"Okay."

"Or seven hundred dollars a month."

"Okay."

He knew I was shopping for office space. He knew how tempting it was to see the perfect spot that was just a little higher in price than what we had budgeted. He knew I would have to look him dead in the eye and justify my extravagance. It was exactly what I needed, and I think we can all use someone like him in our lives!

Thanks to the guidance these men gave me, I was slowly able to adjust my schedule and become more involved in my children's activities.

I respected the honesty and accountability from these men. I grew to love annual planning, and I've made an annual budget ever since. It also helped me see the value of off-site planning. I like the idea of working *on* your business, not just *in* your business. As a result, we take our management team away four times a year for off-site strategy meetings. It's time well spent, and it pays off in the long run.

It was that sort of input and positive growth that allowed me to get more involved in my children's lives. I could leave the office— even during normal business hours if necessary—to join in my kid's activities. In the fall of 1994, Al was in the fourth grade and Preston was in the second grade. Al joined the Boy Scouts and Preston joined the Cub Scouts. To show that I wanted to be more involved, I volunteered to become Preston's den leader, which was a wonderful introduction for me in the world of scouting. Preston and I really enjoyed it, but since Al was in Boy Scouts, not Cub Scouts, it wasn't necessarily doing anything to help the two of us heal our wounds.

Like me, Al was a strong athlete. He was enthusiastic about playing school sports that year, but I had other ideas. Since my parents didn't allow me to play sports until the sixth grade, I decided to impose the same restriction on Al. It became a major rub in our relationship. Thankfully my friend Lonnie helped me see how unfair that limitation was to Al, so by the fifth grade he was heavily involved in football, basketball, and baseball. I tried to help coach his football team that year, but I quickly decided my best bet was to allow other adults to positively influence Al's life. (Plus I really sucked as a coach!)

I moved up with Preston in the scouting program and soon Al, Preston, and I were in the same troop. Allan already had two years of Boy Scouts under his belt, and he was doing well. With me in the troop mix, it could have been trouble. Again, thankfully, another adult, this time Al's scoutmaster, took me aside and suggested, "Let Allan come to Scouts and you turn him over to me. Don't be his father here at Scouts. Leave him alone. Let me be his dad, okay?"

I reluctantly agreed, but it ended up being the best move I could have made. Both Allan and Preston thrived in Scouts, earning the top rank of Eagle Scout. And they each accomplished it one week before their eighteenth birthdays. It probably helped that Trina and I sweetened the pot by proclaiming, "If you achieve Eagle Scout, we will help you buy your first car!" Since only 4 percent of Scouts ever achieve the Eagle rank, I believe that car money was some of the best money we ever spent!

I stayed involved in the world of scouting for a few years after the boys graduated because it once again offered a place for me to influence the lives of young people. As a leader in Scouts, you present the boys with opportunities, and then they do the leading. It's brilliant!

I began to see a role I could have in the lives of boys who had fathers just like me. Young man after young man would walk into the troop with the same story: "My dad is a high-powered, successful businessman who demands that I be successful just like him." For me, it was all about being an affirmative, enriching grown man who could tell those boys, "Hey, you're a good guy! You can do whatever you set your mind to do. Your future is bright!" For them to hear that message from someone other than their dad—and not from a man filled with a critical spirit—had amazing impact.

My relationship with Al was nowhere close to an overnight transformation. The story that opened this book from seventh grade was right in the middle of this transition. In seventh grade Al was ineligible to play athletics and that made a big point in his life. He turned it around in eighth grade—I mean it. At the conclusion of his eighth grade year, Al was awarded Male Athlete of the Year. It was a well-deserved commendation, and we were all so proud of him.

So our relationship grew, but not without continual detours. Two years later, when Al was a sophomore in high school, he decided, against his parent's wishes, to date a girl who happened to be a senior. When I confronted him about it, he was so angry that he picked up a baseball bat and looked like he was ready to use it as a murder weapon.

It was around this time that the family counselor we were talking to suggested the John Wayne/Mr. Rogers material that made a big difference in the way I approached my son. She had one other suggestion that ended up being a real winner as well.

"Dave, I think you and Al should take up a sport together."

"That's a recipe for disaster," I replied in a knee-jerk response.

"I knew you would feel that way, but hear me out," she continued. "The two of you need to take up a sport that you're not good at! It will create some common ground that will help form a real bond between the two of you."

I was willing to try just about anything. So that's how Allan and I began playing golf. And to her credit, our counselor was correct. It became a real bonding experience.

Because we both sucked.

Homes of Hope

In 1997, Trina and I attended a Young Presidents Organization (YPO) Leading by Vision and Values conference in San Diego, California. We were in for a real treat, listening to such world-class speakers as Dr. Bill Bright, Coach Tom Landry, and Rev. Donn Moomaw. None of them disappointed us.

But it was an innocent, quiet lunch with another couple that really changed our lives.

We talked business and leadership, along with the trials and tribulations of being a successful CEO. But before too long, the direction of the conversation changed—radically.

"We've become involved in an annual mission trip just across the border in Mexico," they began their story. "It's one of the most amazing adventures you will ever experience."

"What is it all about?" Trina asked.

"Well, in a nutshell, we go to Mexico for a long weekend, and while we're there, we build five houses from the ground up. When the weekend is concluded, we hand five families the key that unlocks the front door of their new homes."

"Wow!" we exclaimed.

"Of course, these dear people are living in extreme poverty. We've done projects for families who had eighteen or twenty people living in a one-room shanty about the size of a typical bedroom. When they see what we have built for them, it's like they literally see the love of Christ at work in their lives."

"That's pretty awesome," I responded.

"Yes, it is," they replied. "And it is an awesome opportunity for a family to work together on such a meaningful project."

"Family?" Trina interjected as her eyes widened. "Your kids go down there and build with you?"

"That's right."

That was all it took. Trina looked at me dead on and announced, "We need to do this … as a family."

I knew it would be in vain to protest, but I did get one good line in before the decision was made. "Trina, I get camping checked off my list every year by the work I do with the Boy Scouts."

"We're going," she said, "as a family."

"I don't see how this trip will help me in my goal to get to Afghanistan," I sighed, "but count me in."

So with that pivotal luncheon, we began gathering information for the next trip. I discovered the Young Presidents Organization Fellowship Forum offered exactly what we were looking for that December. They called it Homes of Hope, and the project was held just south of San Diego in the tiny Mexican border town of Tijuana. The trip ran from December 28 through the thirtieth—perfectly timed while our kids were on Christmas break from school. It was all coming together.

Since the trip was right after Christmas, we decided to take the money we would normally spend on gifts and put it toward this mission endeavor instead. Trina and I thought that was an excellent idea, but it didn't go over well with a seventh, a fourth, and a second grader. The kids were less than excited, but that would all turn around eventually.

The kids weren't the only ones tentative about this trip. I found myself thinking, "Why am I going on a trip to build something? I'll have to hire someone to repair what I was supposed to build! I'm a software guy, not a hardware guy!" I chuckled as I thought about these personal questions; I assumed God had a sense of humor, and we would all get a good laugh out of my righteous efforts.

On the morning of December 28, we gathered with 116 people on the U.S. side of the border. One hundred twenty people would build five homes in this three-day period. We made the short trek over to Tijuana and listened as the leaders split us up into work teams. Our family was assigned to a team that would build a home for a mom and dad who had five sons. They were living in a shack at the time, so they were excited beyond words. But of course, they didn't know the disadvantage of having me on their team.

We arrived at the construction site, which was a concrete slab. It helped to have the foundation prepared so we could start framing right away. The leaders were so efficient in their plans that the impossible became possible. What was only a cement slab on the first day was a completed home by four p.m. on day two. As long as I live,

I will never forget the look in the eyes of that family when we handed them the key at a dedication ceremony.

I loved it.

Trina loved it.

Our kids loved it.

"I want to do this sort of thing four times a year," Trina said excitedly.

She wasn't exaggerating. The Stone family has participated in over thirty Homes of Hope projects, which averages out to three a year.

Part of the fun for our family was watching me do this type of work. "I'm just so proud of myself that I didn't make any mistakes!" I announced after the first home was completed. Our leader quickly replied.

"You made plenty of mistakes, we just didn't have time to fix them!"

Everyone loved it—especially my kids.

The entire exercise put me in a place where I was no better than anyone else on the project, including my kids. Al, who was in seventh grade at the time, was especially delighted to see his dad messing things up. Al probably goofed up a few things as well, but there was no doubt about it, the Stone Family Mess Up Champion was dear old dad.

For example, I was working on a part of the project where the two gables on the ends of the house needed trusses cut and put in place. "Dave," the project manager called me over to the saw, "I need these two by fours cut into trusses of 22½ inches long. I need nine for each side so that's eighteen total. Got it?"

"Sure thing, boss," I replied.

Regrettably I was a little surer of myself than I should have been. I had all the numbers right; I just didn't have them in the right sequence. Instead of eighteen trusses 22½ inches long, I grabbed the saw, whistled while I worked, and proceeded to cut twenty-two trusses that were 18½ inches long!

One by one I handed them up to the guys on the gables, and they dutifully nailed them into position. It didn't take long to realize I had seriously blown it, since all the trusses were up and there was a huge unexpected gap between the last truss and the gable. We had to cut it all over again, to my chagrin and my kids' delight.

The combination of fun and ministry was absolutely contagious in our family. We helped a family living under a tarp move to a home with a concrete floor, a locked door, and a roof over their head. What an incredible expression of God's mercy!

We still make annual trips to Mexico with YWAM's Homes of Hope team. We have taken friends from our church, employees and their families, as well as customers. It's an amazing way to meet people, minister to them, and leave a long-lasting impact on their lives. My kids have said, "The best taste of God we ever had was our YWAM trips!"

Hiring the Management Team

From the beginning of First Rate our family has always taken the summer as a time to get away. It was always the perfect time of year to escape the Texas heat, visit with our extended family, and spend time with our immediate family while we were on the road. The key phrase in the preceding sentence is "on the road," since we did a lot of this summer travel in everyone's favorite mode of transportation—a motor home, or some call it a recreational vehicle, or RV.

Traveling in an RV allowed me to do some work along the way. We used the travel as an opportunity to visit some of our clients, and I remember well the days of frantically looking for an RV park with phone jacks as one of their amenities so I could connect to the internet through that glorious system known as dial up.

In 1999, at just the time I was looking to get a little bit more out of my leadership team, two of my key leaders, both young women, came to me unbeknownst to each other and requested to have their hours reduced at the company. Both women were married and felt it was the right time to start having children, so they were looking for less responsibility, not more.

Between those two requests and my frequent travel schedule, I decided to make a sweeping change in the organization chart. I wanted to bring in some folks who could provide the management essential for our company, plus have the ability to get out on the road one week a month to meet face-to-face with our customers. So I brought in three guys whom I thought would work well with a fourth guy I already had in place. They became known as the senior management team, each responsible for one of the four departments that made up First Rate.

I hired Terry Gaines to run the products division. I brought in Jeff Kunkel for operations, or what we call application service provider, which was a brand new division at the time. I put Todd Brunskill in charge of consulting. And Craig Wietz ran our service bureau.

My decision to bring in Terry, Jeff, and Todd allowed the two young women, Kate Baird and Debbie Repak, the opportunity to be key contributors while balancing family life. It worked out well for over ten years. After Kate's and Debbie's kids reached high school age, both women stepped back into senior management roles.

I soon discovered this team allowed me the freedom to get away during the summer months, and virtually allowed me total freedom twelve months out of the year. It felt great not to be needed!

We created an environment where we worked together like a big family, we are compensated well, and Dave and Trina are not chained to a desk in Texas! This system has been such a blessing to everyone—most significantly ME! I can go days, weeks, even months without having to be around. Sometimes I don't even know what's going on!

I still play an important role, however. I am the vision caster, especially as it relates to the backbone of our company: technology. I'm also a go-to guy when someone needs problem-solving skills. And I'm constantly brainstorming how to best deliver our products to customers with maximum effectiveness.

For example, one of my proverbs is: "can't just means it hasn't been done yet!" We will find a creative solution that works.

It was not part of the job requirement, but it just so happens that all four of these men are committed Christians. They all subscribe to the value, "I don't want to do work without God in it." And it's working.

As best as I can tell, not many companies use this model. Many presidents feel it is too hands-off. So many business owners think you need a strong manager at the top, but it's not essential for a company to thrive.

Not everyone believes in our model. When I worked with a group of consultants, I posed the questions, "What other companies use a similar model? Whom can we look to for help and encouragement?"

Their answer? "We know of no one else who does it this way. You are a first for us!"

Even one of the members of my board said to me recently, "Admit it, Dave, you're bored and you want out!"

That's not the case at all. I am not bored. We just run things differently.

Our company is made up of highly competent people. We all work very hard. You can count on us; we are trustworthy. And we have one other quality that sets us apart: we are vulnerable. I know many companies who lack transparency, and that lack of vulnerability comes back to hurt them. We know you can be competent, hardworking, and trustworthy, but if you aren't vulnerable it's not going to work.

First Rate offers a safe, non-judgmental, and confidential work environment. We have tried to create a special place for our employees, and everyone tries to create a special working relationship with our clients. As a result, we have enjoyed a profitable run with very high employee satisfaction and client retention.

My Date with Destiny—After Twenty-Four Years!

I love to tell the story of First Rate. Over the years I have had the opportunity to share my story with all types of groups: big ones, small ones, businesses, college students, high school students, churches, community groups, civic groups. I'm not bashful when given the opportunity to show people how the principles of First Rate are really God's principles, and they will work for anyone in any setting.

In October 2001, I was invited to speak to a gathering of Christians meeting in the Northern California town of Chico. They had asked me to tell the story of First Rate, how we made giving back to God an important part of our business, and they asked me to include my personal testimony. I did as I was told and included the part of my life where I felt God had called me to Afghanistan, which I had yet to fulfill.

After the meeting a gentleman approached me and whispered, "We have friends in central Asia. They will go into Afghanistan after the war ends."

"That's very interesting," I calmly replied, my attention piqued. His next statement floored me.

"Would you like to go with them?"

Fortunately the chaplain of First Rate at the time—a fine man named Wayne Hamit—was with me and overheard the entire conversation. He knew how important an offer like this one was to me. Wayne stepped forward and collected further information about this prospective trip. We discovered the organization had staff members in Afghanistan prior to 9/11, and they were planning to return once the war was over. A meeting was planned for late 2001 in Colorado to discuss a trip to Afghanistan in the spring of 2002. Wayne and I discussed the opportunity and decided he would attend the meeting and potentially make the first trip into Afghanistan, which is exactly what happened.

Wayne went to Afghanistan in April 2002. Upon his return I was anxious to hear his assessment. As a former Navy chaplain, Wayne understood the full spectrum of issues regarding this endeavor.

"So, what did you think?" I asked. His answer was short and to the point.

"Dave, we've got to do it!"

"Wow, you sound pretty certain about this idea," I replied.

"I do," he answered. "The next trip is scheduled for later this year—in August."

August? I thought to myself. That would make my entrance into Afghanistan exactly twenty-four years from when God had told me I would be going there!

The method our friends used to get into the country was creative, helpful, and perfectly legal. They go in as a non-governmental organization, or NGO for short. They do relief and development work with and for the people of the country. I was filled with every emotion possible the day we left. I knew the Lord had set this trip in motion, but I couldn't help but feel nervous, as well as confused. *How are You going to use me on this trip, Lord?* I prayed over and over.

The height of emotion occurred the day we arrived in Uzbekistan in preparation for our journey across the border to neighboring Afghanistan. Our American host ran an NGO in Uzbekistan, so he was aware of what awaited us. He walked us to a train bridge, which looked to be about two or three hundred yards across. It is called the Friendship Bridge, joining Uzbekistan with Afghanistan. It didn't feel friendly to me as Wayne and I joined our host in walking across the bridge. The Uzbeks are formerly a part of the Soviet Union, and to say it is an oppressive environment is an understatement.

As the three of us prepared to cross the bridge, the Uzbek guards watched our every move, guns at the ready. As we approached their checkpoint, a misunderstanding occurred regarding my camera. Not speaking the language, I was ready to hand over my Sony to an Uzbek guard, when he suddenly thrust it back in my hands and waved us on our way.

We finally passed the Uzbekistan side of the border and the emotional release was unbelievable; I can still feel the energy bursting out of every pore of my body. It was my moment with destiny—a date I had anticipated for twenty-four years. As I marched across the bridge with my small suitcase on wheels packed with clothes for the next two weeks, I could no longer contain myself, and I began to weep freely.

Once we were on the other side of the bridge, an Afghan guard with a rifle slung over his shoulder met us. Rather than his gun at the ready, this man stepped forward and hugged our host, then Wayne, and then me. He smiled broadly and warmly greeted us, "Welcome! Thank you for coming to Afghanistan!" It was night and day in contrast to life on the Uzbek side. After more hugs and a few photos, the warm Afghan hospitality continued and we made our way through Customs. An American working for an NGO was supposed to pick us up at the border, but he was running late, so we waited. I still didn't know what to expect, but I was trying to absorb it all.

Before too long a Toyota Forerunner created a trail of dust as it made its way to our locale. We hopped in, greeted one another, and began a four-hour drive deep into the desert. It was about 110 degrees as we headed out into the sand. About twenty minutes into our journey, we slowly came to a halt. The dunes were so big that giant earthmovers had to clear the sand on the road. However, the earthmovers were broken; therefore, there was a truck stuck in the road, and we were all stuck behind him. I noticed that some vehicles attempted to drive off the side of the road and make a go of it on the sand. But none got very far before spinning their wheels in the deep desert sand. Plus no one knew exactly where landmines were buried, so going off road was not without danger.

When someone was stuck in the sand, everyone got out of his car or truck to help. No unwilling bystanders. Everyone was on board.

I didn't know what was going to happen to us, but I could tell the Afghans were helpful people and everything was going to be okay. Eventually our driver tried the off-road maneuver, and like everyone else, we got stuck. Yet people freely lent a hand, and we finally got going. After a long wait, we inched around the traffic snarl. Three hours later we made it to the NGO.

It was dusk and I found myself thinking about what would have happened if we had been stuck in the sand overnight? It has certainly happened to others. But God spared us that drama.

We arrived in Sheberghan, which was home to the NGO known as Crosslink Development International. At CDI's offices and guesthouse, we met additional staff and took a quick tour of the CDI complex. The two-story building had an office and dining area downstairs and a guesthouse for sleeping upstairs. We slept on long pillows called toshaks. They measure approximately two feet wide by seven feet long. If you sleep on your side you can stay on top of one; otherwise, you sleep with one by your side!

There was no running water in the house so a shower consisted of two buckets of water: one to wash yourself down and one to rinse yourself off. We used a squeegee to get everything as dry as possible. There was a sink, but again, no running water accompanying it. The toilet was called a squatty potty. You stood on footrests and squatted. A bucket of water sat next to the footrests to wash down whatever was done. All of it took some getting used to, but it's amazing how quickly you can adapt.

CDI had a separate building where the kitchen was located. A cook prepared our meals as we assembled in the dining area. We sat on long pillows surrounding a plastic tablecloth placed on the floor. Here's my assessment of the food we ate: FANTASTIC! I loved the way we ate. We were served lots of rice, grapes, melons, tomatoes, peppers, and an assortment of other fruits and vegetables. They offered a small amount of chicken and some french fries; we drank tea all of the time. Some of the best bread I've ever tasted accompanied every meal. They would bake a flatbread, which was served warm, right out of the oven. We slathered it with butter and jam, and the taste was outstanding. We ate fruit, eggs, and flatbread for breakfast and then kabobs for lunch and dinner. I truly enjoyed it.

We met workers in Sheberghan who were expatriates from Brazil, Australia, the United States, and of course some Afghans. One of the projects of CDI was to drill freshwater wells. They created the wells by using a drill mechanism connected to a truck. They taught the community how to drill and maintain the well. Typically it took a week to create a well thirty meters deep. We learned that a week was considered slow going in comparison to some of the other agencies, but the CDI was committed to teaching the Afghans how to keep the well up and running, which added to the timeframe. This was a major philosophical difference with most of the other NGO's in the area. CDI saw itself as a developmental type of organization, thus the important teaching component. Most other groups saw themselves as relief organizations. They felt the most effective way to operate was drilling the most wells in the shortest amount of time. The fallacy in that strategy was that in thirty to ninety days the well would break and no one would know how to fix it. It didn't take too long for those wells to shut down or become contaminated. "Fast is slow and slow is fast," David Stillwell taught me, a valuable insight.

I also learned the importance of keeping my mouth shut. Early in our visit, I tried to make jokes with some of the expatriates and my humor fell flat. My attempt at comedy in the Afghan world bombed. "Listen more and speak less," David told me. "You will learn a great deal more that way." I began to see the importance of being an observer as opposed to a wisecracking, "have a great time!" kind of guy. For me, the entire trip was about learning how to share my spiritual journey in a cross-cultural setting. It was about learning their ways, giving up my ways, plus giving up my right to do it my way.

Clothing was another area of life where I had some learning and adapting to do. I discovered quickly that men do not wear short pants, and they never take their shirts off. It is completely inappropriate to do so in their culture. I also grew a beard, a more appropriate look for an older man. Most men wore sandals, a pair of drawstring pants, a long shirt, and a vest. Turbans were also common for men, but I have yet to start wearing one of those!

Since I didn't pack drawstring pants or a vest, I had to find a way to acquire the traditional Afghan garb. It was an amazing process, beginning with a visit to a fabric store to purchase cloth. Then we walked five doors down to a tailor who measured me and told me that I could pick up my new clothes the next day! To top it off, this dear tailor was so grateful that we were in his country to help that he offered me his lunch. What an act of gratitude! I discovered he was representative of the majority of Afghan people I met—kind, humble, and grateful.

Once I was settled, I explored the business community. I was clearly viewed as "The American Business Guy" so I used it to my advantage. "Let's pay a visit to the Ministry of Commerce so we can find out how businesses operate around here," I announced one morning. A man dressed in Western clothes, who was anxious to help, met with us. "Would you like to meet the richest business men in town?" he asked after we had chatted for a bit.

"Sure," I replied, "I'd love to."

Fifteen minutes later, in walks Haji Jon. He was the sort of man who commanded your attention. He was a handsome, well-groomed, stately man in his sixties; I was most impressed with the beautiful cape he wore. Haji Jon had left Afghanistan during the reign of the Taliban, but he had returned home after the Taliban had been overthrown. He was warm and friendly to me.

"Come to my place of business," he invited. "We will talk and drink tea."

"I'd like that," I responded, and off we went.

Once at his business, we sat on pillows and sipped tea. Eventually Haji Jon asked me the big question: "So, Mr. Stone, exactly why are you here in my country?"

I answered honestly, "I am here to share the love of God and to help raise up a portion of Afghanistan that is godly. God told me I am supposed to do this. And He told me that twenty-four years ago."

Haji was fascinated with my answer. "So what is it that you do as your business?" he asked.

"I am in the computer software business," I replied.

"Interesting."

"Yes, it is an interesting business. You might also find it interesting to know that we give away ten percent of our revenue every year."

Haji Jon raised his eyebrows in surprise. "I have a friend who lives in New York City who gave away a great deal of money in order to build a mosque in the city."

"Giving is an important principle to us in our business," I replied.

"You are a fascinating man, Mr. Stone," Haji smiled as he spoke. "I would like to invite you to my home for dinner tomorrow evening. I have some friends that I would like you to meet."

The next evening was a memorable occasion.

This was no small dinner get-together. Forty to fifty people showed up at Haji's home. Wayne and I watched in amazement as these men conversed. Some of the Afghan guests had been run out of the country by the Taliban. To make it really interesting, other men in attendance were former Taliban. In other words, the room was filled with a group of people who once were bitter enemies. Wayne and I couldn't understand a single word they said; there was no interpreter.

Sitting in their midst, I had no idea how they felt. For us, it was a quiet evening—mostly smiles and an occasional grunt or groan. One gentleman was particularly taken by the three Americans, especially Wayne. We found out it wasn't Wayne so much as his wristwatch! The Afghan was so gaga over it that Wayne finally offered it to his new friend.

By silently observing, we could see who the lighthearted guys were and who the serious guys were. The nonverbal communication told us a lot about the real story. Who knows what was going outside of Haji's dining room, but the message that evening was unity.

Haji was the consummate host, and as we all left his home, he made a point of saying, "Mr. Stone, please come and see me again."

Part of the reason we traveled to Afghanistan was to explore a proposal we had received from the Women's Council regarding a plan to teach women how to make carpets. Would the NGO and First Rate be interested in underwriting a training center, as well as purchasing looms, hand tools, materials, teacher salaries, etc.? We said we would consider it, and once we arrived, it did look like a good idea from our perspective. I just needed a little more convincing to be certain. And that's when I had the idea. I turned to Wayne and said, "Let's go ask Haji!"

"This is a good skill for women to learn," Haji began, once he heard about our idea. "It is a good thing for the Women's Council to teach women. I like it."

"I am so glad to hear that," I said.

"How many looms do they want to purchase?" he asked curiously.

"They want twenty looms," I replied. "They want ten of them to be steel looms for higher quality carpets and the other ten can be wooden looms for lesser quality."

It was at that point that Haji began speaking in more excited tones. Between his energized voice and the shocked look on our translator's face, we were dying to know what he was saying.

"This man is rich because he is not a nice man," our translator said to us—obviously not what Haji was saying. "He is a harsh businessman. He doesn't care about anyone else at all." And then he added, "What he is saying has dumbfounded me!"

"So what is he saying?" I begged him to tell me.

The translator looked at me in disbelief and answered. "Haji does not want you to buy the looms. He wants to donate the twenty looms for the training center!"

Now we were shocked!

"He says that he will donate the twenty looms and you can buy the materials," the translator continued. "He says that he wants to be your partner!"

I smiled and nodded at Haji. He invited me to walk with him outside where he showed me the looms he used in his business. He would make certain the training center received looms of the best quality.

I went back to my room that evening overwhelmed by the wonderful picture of how the Lord could use me. The way we do business with the community back in the United States is how people can work together all over the world.

Haji had caught the spirit of giving. We learned later he had sent rice to the local orphanage while we were there. It was the beginning of a truly remarkable partnership. Unfortunately it only lasted a year. Haji turned his business over to his son, who did not share Haji's spirit of giving. But nonetheless it was perhaps the most memorable moment of my trip.

My time in Afghanistan was remarkable, but it was only the beginning for me. I have been back twice a year for the last seven years. In those visits I have learned two very important lessons.

First, I learned how to be an appropriate friend to the people of that country. Being appropriate means that I regularly remind myself to shut up and listen. Just being a friend and a listener makes a huge impact in the lives of the people with whom I come in contact. Even though more and more partnerships are being created between the Afghans and the Americans, visitors from the States are most welcomed.

All I do is drink tea and listen. It's amazing how much that means to them. One of the expat single women I met there has no father or brother, so I have become her "filter" so men know she has a man in her life looking out for her like a big brother. I take it seriously—so much so that I have had long distance phone conversations with her prospective suitors.

The second lesson I learned concerns the influence I can have in the business world. I *can* be nice, godly, and successful in business.

Just like people took to our style in the United States, the same principles worked in Afghanistan. When I am invited to tell the First Rate story, I often ask audiences, "If you could take God to work, what would it look like? What does it mean to bring God into the workplace? What does it mean to live our entire lives before the face of God?" Some folks appear shocked that I would even raise such a subject. It's like they live with the idea that people will conduct business as if God is not looking. Without that sort of accountability, trouble is not far behind. I want to live a life that honors God, both at work and at home. Onstage and backstage. I want my clients to see it just like I want my wife and children to see it. It has been a longtime coming, but God is helping me achieve my dream.

He can help you achieve yours as well. Get Him in the mix right away and be prepared for a life like you've never before experienced.

I like to call it First Rate Living.